Signs of the Season

SPRING

Published by Happy Crab Press, a trade name of Happy Crab Corp., P.O. Box 1329, Laporte, CO 80535, a Colorado not-for-profit corporation.

Printed in the United States of America.

Written & illustrated by: Sally Roth
Editor and consultant: Matthew Bartmann
Cover design: Matthew Bartmann
Cover photos: Matthew Bartmann

Contact Sally and Matt: Join us on Facebook! We'd love to see you! Or email us at sparrow@sallyroth.com.
Sally's Facebook page: www.facebook.com/sally.roth.12
"Nature Ramblings with Sally Roth & Matt Bartmann" Facebook page:
www.facebook.com/SallyRothandMattBartmann
Sally's website: www.sallyroth.com

ABOUT THE COVER
Signs of spring! Iconic daffodil in center of front cover, with (clockwise) tufted titmouse, spring blue butterfly, morel mushroom, and fire pink (*Silene virginica*) wildflower. Back cover, house wren and Sally the Turtle Saver . All photos © 2017 Matthew Bartmann.

Signs of the Season

SPRING

Written & illustrated by SALLY ROTH

HAPPY CRAB PRESS

WELCOME, SPRING!

Spring is a season of firsts: First robin, first wild-flower, first morel mushroom...the firsts keep coming all through the season.

By the calendar, spring begins on or around March 20—the moment of Vernal Equinox, when the Equator is tilted toward the sun, and day and night are of equal length.

But the natural world doesn't wait until then to start shifting into the new season.

Signs of spring start in late winter, and keep going through May, for a large part of the country.

For others (Hi, us, here in the high Rockies!), spring is a late bloomer, starting two months behind even when the calendar says it should.

In the South and other mild climates, signs of spring start showing up as early as late January.

So when is spring, exactly?

Listen to your birds as family time begins, keep an eye out for migrants (oh boy, vultures! Oh boy, hummingbirds!), watch the plants and trees in your garden and in wild places, and you'll get a feel for the *real* cycle of the seasons.

Oh boy—it's *SPRING!*

Sally Roth

EARLY SPRING

The dates of what counts as "early spring" generally run from mid-February through March, in many regions. But in warmer places, early spring can kick off in January; in colder regions (hello, high Rockies!), even the earliest signs of spring may not appear until May.

Instead of going by the calendar, use your eyes and ears to see how Nature is moving along. That way, you won't miss a moment!

How Do You Say That Again?

I rarely say the word "harbinger" out loud, and I never can remember whether it's harbinger with a hard g, or harbinjer (just checked; it's harbinjer). But it's a word I love to read or write, if the words "of spring" follow it. Yay! Spring!

Don't Rely on Robins

Who's the most famous harbinger of spring? The robin, of course. But robins get way more glory than they deserve as the harbinger of spring. Why? Because many of them stick around all winter!

Hardly a Harbinger

If you have lingering crabapples, holly, hawthorn, or other berries in your neighborhood, you may see robins even in the depths of winter. No, you didn't see the first robin back in January—that was one of the bunch that stuck around.

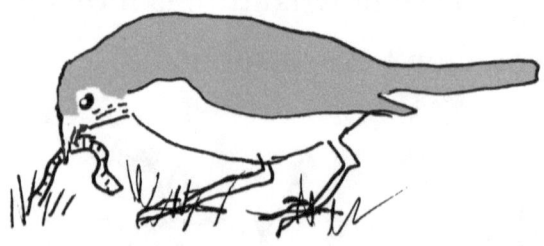

Habits Reveal the Harbinger

A flock of robins, or even a lone bird, hopping about on your lawn, head cocked to one side and listening? Absolutely a sign of spring! That behavior means worms are up.

Wiggly Migration

Worms migrate downward past the frost line to wait out the winter, then make their way back to near the surface only when the soil warms up. Yahoo! Spring!

Hark, The Herald!

Birdsong starts slowly, with resident winter birds being the first to feel their oats as the days start to lengthen in earliest spring. Spend a few minutes outside in the morning, even on the coldest days, and you'll hear the difference.

The Change in Chickadees

Chickadees are one of the first singers, adding a sweet whistled "*fee-bee*" to their dee-dee-dee chatter. Spring is on the way!

The Symbol of Love

Doves, of course, and they start cooing even before Valentine's Day, when their image is bound to decorate a greeting card. Or, more likely nowadays, a Facebook meme.

Screaming Doves

Listen for the quiet "*Ah-coo-cooo*" of mourning doves, and the weird screaming as well as cooing of the Eurasian collared dove, an introduced species that's now spread like wildfire across much of the country.

Singing Star

Love 'em or hate 'em, starlings are great singers. Listen for their rich, varied, melodic warbling while you're outside caulking up those holes in the soffits they're eyeing as a possible home—they're one of the earliest singers.

Out of Step

My very first column for a newspaper, some 30 years ago, was about how to coax forsythia into early bloom.

I asked my son to read it and tell me his opinion. "It's fun to read, Mom, but, um… everybody has fake flowers nowadays."

Huh.

Real Is...Well, REAL

Guess I've always been out of step with the mainstream, because, to my mind, even a single dandelion flower beats the most sumptuous bouquet of silk flowers by a mile.

Give Spring a Nudge

Nothing gladdens a winter-weary heart like a bunch of fresh flowers! So clip branches from your yard to bring inside—the warmth will nudge them into bloom in a hurry.

Zoom into Bloom

The earlier a shrub or tree blooms outside in spring, the quicker it will be to open its buds indoors.

Best Candidates

For the quickest gratification, stick to forsythia, pussywillows, and a personal favorite, maple trees of any kind (not Japanese maples, though; they're slowpokes).

Consider the Wait

Yes, you can force lilacs and dogwood, but boy, it's a long wait. By the time your bouquet begins to open, daffodils could be blooming outside.

How Long Until They Bloom?

Figure on about 3 to 4 weeks until flowers, for forsythia and flowering quince; 2 to 3 weeks for pussywillows.

ALL Willows Are Pussywillows!

Catkins are the flowers of willows, and every single species produces them, early in spring. Before those catkins elongate and produce pollen, they're sweet tightly furred buds. Pussywillows, in other words!

Forsythia
Sprig

Go for the Big Guys

Not all pussywillows are created equal—some are tiny, some are skinny, some are sparse. All are gratifying to force into bloom inside, but those with bigger buds are the most attention-getting in the garden. Look for pink and black varieties, too, for a change of pace.

Pussywillows with a Twist

Check the fresh flowers section of your supermarket or ask a florist for a few stems of fresh, not dried, "curly willow," a popular accent in bouquets.

Everlasting Pussywillows

Put pussywillows in a vase without water, or dump out the water when your "forced" ones bloom, and they'll hold in that stage for decades! The stem itself will shrivel as it dries and stiffens, but the silvery buds will stay well attached, and looking good.

Natural Landmark

My grandparents had a huge house that was scary to a little kid trying to find her way around. But inside was a landmark that helped me find my way—two huge turquoise-blue urns in a hallway that held pussywillows about 8 feet tall. Yay! No longer lost!

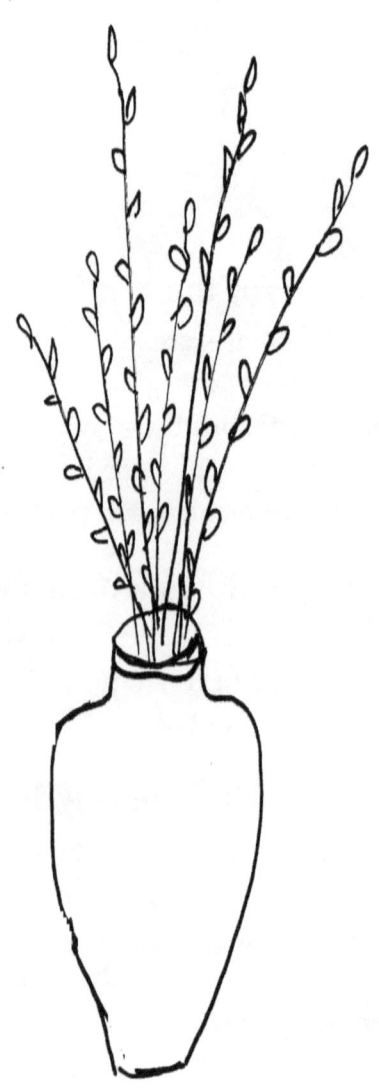

And A Rubber Ducky?

Some of my garden writer colleagues like to overcomplicate things. "Submerge the stems in a bathtub of warm water," they advise, when giving instructions for coaxing snipped stems of forsythia and others into early bloom.

Common Sense—or Laziness

Are you kidding me? Who wants to bend over a tub, shoving clippings under water, let alone wipe all those bits of bark and buds out of the tub? Not me, thank you!

Skip the Bath

Yes, a tub soak will quicken the process by a couple of days, but no, I do not give my stems a bath. I just stick them into a jar or vase of warm water. They always bloom soon enough for me!

An-ti-ci-pa-a-tion

In a week or two, you'll see the buds expanding, and then it'll be about few days, depending on how warm your house is, until the actual flower buds start to peep out. Oh boy, the first glimpse of color, so exciting!

Big Blast of Spring

Years ago, a friend of mine coaxed a huge amount of forsythia into bloom for her late-winter wedding, filling 5 gallon buckets with hundreds of clippings. It made an incredible show!

One Is Enough

No need to go whole hog like that, though—a single stem is all you need to supply that oh-so-welcome taste of spring.

Not a Robin

The first sight of a towhee at the feeder often stumps backyard birdwatchers. "Looks sort of like a robin with those orangeish sides, but isn't a robin..." Nope. It's a towhee, a bird that usually sticks to thick brush or woods.

Out of the Woods

In spring, though, a towhee or two often shows up in backyards, scratching for spilled seed.

Females Can Fool You

Female towhees are even bigger foolers than males. Males have a lot of black on their heads and backs, but females are brown instead—even more robin-like. They're one of the most notorious for fooling feeder-watchers, because we usually only get to see them in early spring.

Drink Your Teeeee

Many folks translate the towhee's song to "Drink your teeeee..." It's a great match, in terms of accent and pitch. But towhees have another call, which they give all year.

Have Some WHEAT!

The towhee's most frequent call is when it says its name, but not as you might expect it to be pronounced: Not "toe-hee," not "toe-wheee," not "toey," but an emphatically ended *"toe-WHEET!"*

Was That a Chewink I Just Heard?

The towhee was once known as the chewink, a name that comes closer to its distinctive two-note call. Just be sure to put the accent on the *wink*.

Towhee

A Mist of Color

The new green of tree leaves is glorious, but we're not at that stage yet. Gradually, very gradually, the color of those trees begins to change. You'll notice it best when you look at a woods ore a single tree from a distance.

First Blush

Not green yet, but a warm rusty to reddish haze, depending on what kind of trees you're looking at. Once you see that rosy mist, it'll only be a few weeks until spring green.

All Wrapped Up

Leaf buds are on tree branches all through winter. Take a look at any tree's buds in December, and they'll be closed up tight, infant leaves or flowers-to-be wrapped within sturdy bud scales.

Oh Boy! Buds Are Swelling!

By late winter, those buds are expanding, because the baby leaves or flowers inside are getting bigger. "Aspen buds are getting bigger!"

Getting Ready to Pop

One fine early spring day, the bud scales can no longer hold back the tide: They pop open, and the first tiny leaves or, in the case of maples, fuzzy flowers unfold.

Backyard Barometer

Silver maples were sold by the millions thanks to ads in Sunday newspaper magazines that touted them as fast-growing shade trees. One may be growing near you, and it's a great barometer of spring!

Silver maple flowers

Silver to Red

The bark of silver maple twigs is silvery, but the buds are a warm red that's beautiful against a blue sky. You'll have to look up, way up, to appreciate the scene, because silver maples grow 80 feet tall.

First Flowers of Spring

If you have a silver maple in your neighborhood, congratulations on being able to watch for one of the earliest flowers of spring! Silver maples open their flowers even before the first crocus peeps its head up.

Fuzzy Flowers

Maples of all types have fuzzy bumbles of flowers studding their twigs or hanging in clusters, and all bloom early. The fuzzy appearance is created by a mass of thin stamens.

Fooled by the Sun

Warm sunshine pulls honeybees from their hives in search of nectar long before bountiful flowers are blooming.

The first bees scout out nectar sources, then come back to tell others in the hive which way to go.

Flowers Indeed

Those bees may not be too early after all, because chances are the warm sun *has* brought flowers into bloom, just not yet in the garden.

Earlybird Special!

Early blooming maples, especially silver maples, are a vital source of nectar and pollen for early-flying honeybees.

Spot the Seekers

Watch the top branches of a blooming maple tree with binoculars, and you're likely to have honeybees cross your view.

Often, the tree is attended by lots of honeybees, all busy gathering nectar at the fuzzy flowers.

Humming with Bees

Listen—can you hear that hum? That's the sound of bee wings busy at work. Amazing, isn't it!

A Saucer of Sweetness

It's easy to set up a "bee feeder" in very early spring, when flowers are scarce. Pour out a pool of honey on a saucer, and you can watch the bees eagerly dab it up!

Busy as Bees

It's fun to feed bees. And don't worry, they'll be so intent on eating that they're no threat to watchers. The handout can really help them out, too, when flowers are few and far between.

Fool Me Once, Fool Me Twice...

I'm embarrassed to admit how many years I listened to tufted titmice without realizing whose voice I was hearing. I'd whistle back to that loud *"PETER! PETER! PETER!"*, but the only bird that ever came in sight was a tufted titmouse, far too small for such a big voice. Duh.

Go Ahead, Snicker

I usually say "titmouse" without a qualm when I'm talking to other bird lovers; we all automatically think "little gray bird with a crest" when we hear the name. But to non-birdwatchers, the name is good for a snicker...or, should we say, titter.

All Sorts of Tits

In England, "tit" means a small bird, and should you explore British birds, you'll find blue tits, coal tits, marsh tits, willow tits, crested tits, and snicker-inducing great tits.

Help for Early honeybees!

American Tits

Our tits include only three kinds of little birds: the titmice (tufted, bridled, oak, juniper); the wrentit of California, and the bushtit of the West.

Spotting a Foreigner

British tits—the birds, the birds—are as common and abundant at feeders as our chickadees, but they're more colorful. So American magazines and catalogs often use photos of them in ads for feeders and feeder foods, or to illustrate bird articles or books.

Gotcha!

Do a quick online search for "bird tit" (be sure to include that word "bird," or you'll see pictures you'd be happier not seeing!), and take a look at the foreign species—that way, you'll know when a photo comes from a British backyard, not an American one. Oops!

Up Through the Snow

I love science, because it explains all those things I've noticed and wondered why about. Skunk cabbage, for instance, whose spears of furled leaves emerge in boggy places while there's still deep snow or even ice.

Mitosis Makes Heat

Every cell in those rapidly expanding skunk cabbage shoots creates a tiny bit of heat as it divides and multiplies. That cell activity creates enough warmth to send the new shoot right up through ice and snow, melting it as it grows.

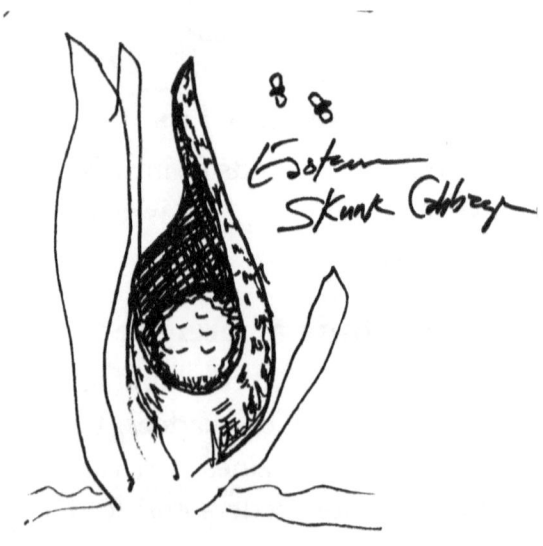

That's a Flower?

The pretty colors we think of at the word "flowers" sure aren't evident in eastern skunk cabbage, whose spike of tiny flowers wears a hood, or spathe, of unappealing murky red-brown.

Calling All Flies

Unappealing to us, that is—to flies, it's just the ticket, signaling, oh boy, rotting flesh! Dried blood! Yum!

Flies Are Pollinators, Too

When skunk cabbage blooms, early spring flies come quick, pollinating the flower as they buzz around searching for their favorite (nonexistent) food.

Lighting up the Swamp

The hood over the flower of western skunk cabbage is a totally different color than the dead-meat hue of eastern skunk cabbage—it's bright buttery yellow, so pretty that the plant was brought to Europe as a bog-garden gem.

Tit for Tat

Once outside of its native home, in those European gardens, western skunk cabbage spread like lightning. It's now on the European invasive species list…just as purple loosestrife, a pretty European wetland plant, is on ours.

Skunk Smell

I actually like the smell of skunk perfume, and the very similar aroma of skunk cabbage leaves. And to me the tiny flowers under that colorful hood—if you can get down low enough to give them a sniff—smell deliciously sweet. Apparently my nose is weird, because to most folks, skunk is a stench.

Raspberry or Strawberry?

Telling purple finches and house finches apart can be tricky, so be prepared to take a closer look if the purple guys show up at your feeder in early spring, as they are

wont to do. Most noticeable clue: Purple finches are pur-
pler than house finches—dipped in raspberry juice, as
Roger Tory Peterson said, rather than strawberry.

Look at the Females

If you still can't decide which finch you have, look for a
female. Purple finch females have a wide, whitish stripe
above the eye that stands out like a sore thumb. No instantly noticeable stripe? House finch.

The Nose Knows

For a surefire way to determine which finch you're hosting,
look at the shape of the bill. Is the top of the bill curved
downward to the tip? House finch. Does the top of the bill
go down on a straight line to the tip? Purple.

Leapfrog in the Moonlight

Early spring is mating season for cottontails, and courtship
"dances" are part of the process. Look out your window
on a moonlit night, and you may see bunnies leapfrogging
over each other as they pair off to make more bunnies.

Not So Friendly

Some of those leaping rabbits may be fighting with other.
Males battle over territory and females, just as other animals do. Charging each other is a popular tactic.

Deadly Audience

Owls are fully aware of leaping bunnies, as well as of
night-feeding bunnies who creep out to nibble on twigs or
greenery under cover of dark. If the moonlight is bright
enough, scan the tops of utility poles or trees with binoculars, for the silhouette of an owl.

House Finch   Purple Finch

Making a Family...Fast!

Pregnancy lasts only 28 days in cottontails. Four weeks after birth, the youngsters are on their own—and at 2 to 3 months of age, they're able to breed.

Doing the Math

If we figure that each female cottontail raises 3 to 4 litters a year, starting in early spring, with an average number of five "kits," that's 15 new bunnies in the world from one female alone.

Breeding Like Rabbits

If half of that first set of cottontail offspring are female, and all of them breed twice that same year, that's 40 new rabbits. Add the 15 of the original batch, and that's 55 offspring from the original female in a single year!

Bye-bye, Extra Bunnies

Good thing just about every predator out there— hawks, owls, weasels, foxes, coyotes, bobcats, and let's not forget house cats—loves to eat bunnies. Otherwise, we'd be wading through an ocean of rabbits.

All Kinds of Cottontails

The eastern cottontail (*Sylvilagus floridanus*) covers the whole eastern half of the country.

But it has plenty of relatives: the mountain cottontail (*Sylvilagus nuttalli*) in the High Rockies where we live,, plus the New England cottontail (*Sylvilagus transitionalis*); and another half-dozen species fill other niches in America, from marshes to forests to deserts.

Joy in the Mourning

The first butterfly of spring is almost always a mourning cloak. This mid-sized butterfly sleeps beneath flaps of bark in winter, emerging at the first spell of warm days.

Sign of Respect

The mourning cloak gets its name from its deep umber brown color, which looks black from a distance, the only acceptable color for mourning clothes back in the old days.

Psst—Your Slip Is Showing

The creamy white edging on a mourning cloak's wings always reminds me of the lace of an old-fashioned petticoat peeking out under the gloomy cloak.

Nice touch, even if it is a trifle lighthearted for mourning clothes!

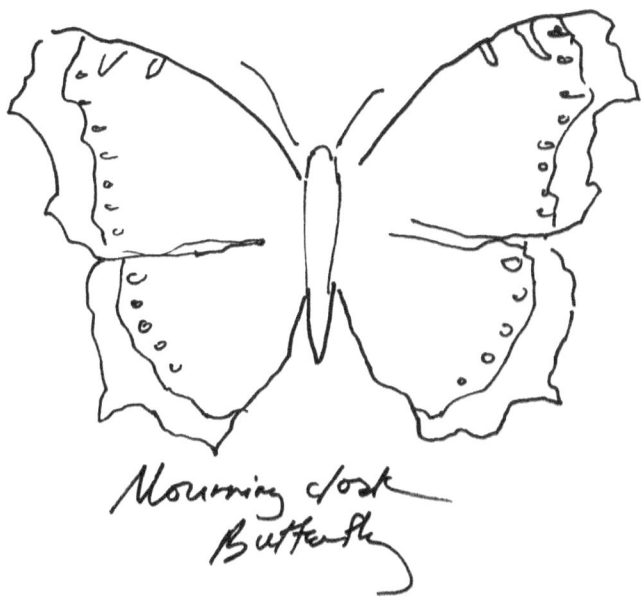

Mourning cloak
Butterfly

Sipping Sap

Mourning cloaks visit early flowers (Virginia bluebells were a favorite in my former Indiana yard), but they'll also seek out sap to get their nourishment. Look for the butterfly fluttering near trees or in the woods, as well as at flowers.

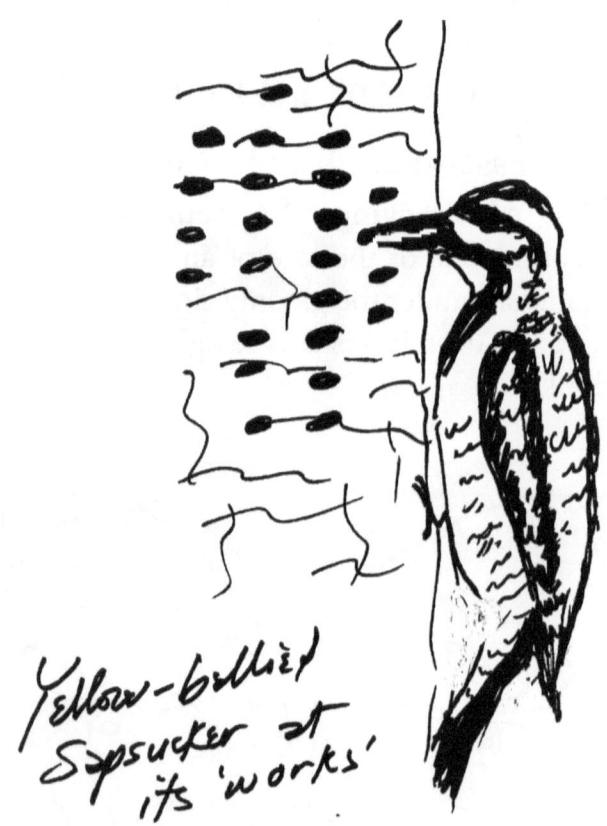

Yellow-bellied Sapsucker at its 'works'

Filling the Well

The yellow-bellied sapsucker is no joke, and neither are its cousins, the red-naped, red-breasted, and Williamson's. All drill a grid of holes in trees—the sap "works" that they return to again and again as the holes fill with sweet stuff and collect yummy insects.

Another Sort of "Cat Bird"

Listen for the mewing cry of the yellow-bellied sapsucker in early spring, when the birds return from their winter vacations in the Southeast and Central America. Sounds a lot like a kitty's breathy meow.

Hummingbird Helper

Hummingbirds depend on sapsucker works when they return, especially in northern areas or after a late spring cold snap. Flowers can be few and far between then, but sap is always available, thanks to hardworking sapsuckers.

Dinner Is Served

Just like everything in Nature, the timing is perfect—sapsuckers return about a few weeks before hummers, giving them plenty of time to drill their wells and get the

Red-naped Sapsucker

sap flowing to fill them. Hummers drink the sap and get a nifty bonus of protein by dabbing up the insects at it.

Spice Up Your Yard

I can't say enough good things about spicebush (*Lindera benzoin*), a native shrub that grows in eastern and Midwestern woods. Its yellow bumbles of insect-attracting flowers bloom before the leaves, early in spring, lighting up the woods—or your shady garden.

Where to Get It

Spicebush is easy to transplant from your own or a friend's woods. Even larger specimens—4 to 6 feet tall—usually take only a few minutes of digging and levering to loosen the shallow roots. It's also sold online, and at some native plant nurseries.

Four Seasons of Beauty

Spicebush is one of the most gracefully shaped bushes you'll ever see, with dark, curving branches that are beautiful in winter. In summer, its leaves are the preferred food of spicebush swallowtail caterpillars. Glossy red fall berries beckon thrushes and bluebirds.

Smells Like Ben-Gay

Smash a leaf of spicebush in your fingers, and you'll get a whiff of a delicious aromatic scent. Delicious if you like the scent of Ben-Gay, that is, because that's exactly what spicebush smells like.

A Relative Newcomer

Forsythia is in so many of our yards, you might think it's been around forever (and it has, in its native China), but it was only introduced to the western world in 1844, when plant hunter Robert Fortune brought it back to England.

A Little Too Late

Forsythia was named in honor of William Forsyth, the Scottish gardener of King George III and a founder of the Royal Horticultural Society. The sad part? Forsyth never saw his namesake plant—he was long dead by the time it came to England.

The Good Old Days

Uh oh, I'm a geezer now for sure—I often catch myself saying "Remember when…" or "Whatever happened to…"

Times have sure changed in the gardening world, with nearly all plants, except for trees, being sold in pots these days.

Whatever Happened to Bareroot Bundles?

Back in the day, it was bareroot bundles for familiar shrubs—hedge privet, forsythia, pussywillows—and boy, were they cheap! All are super-easy to root from cuttings, and that's exactly what you were buying—rooted cuttings.

Feel Like Gambling?

A very, very few catalogs (usually printed on newsprint paper, not glossy pages) still sell old-favorite shrubs in bundles, but most of those sellers are not known for reliability. Still, if you spot a great buy…. Yeah, I can't resist, either!

Be Patient

You'll get what looks like a bunch of dead sticks if you buy bareroot shrubs by mail, but once in moist soil, they'll come back like Lazarus if they still have even a slight bit of life left in them. And wait'll you see how fast they grow!

Eastern bluebird pair
Note the "hunched"
posture

The Fingernail Test

To tell whether dormant mail-order trees or shrubs are alive or dead, scrape off a bit of bark with your thumbnail. If it's green underneath, they're alive.

Dead and Brown

If it's tan underneath the bark, and twigs are brittle and easily snap clean off, it's most likely dead as a doornail. Time to call customer service.

Best Beloved Blues!

Beautiful and good-natured, bluebirds are slower moving than most birds, so they're great fun to watch. In cold regions, they're early migrants who return when snow is still on the ground and spring blizzards are in the offing. In more hospitable regions, they're around all year.

Welcome Home

Bluebirds dine at our offerings for long minutes at a time, instead of using the "grab and go" method of chickadees, nuthatches, and many other feeder birds. Be ready with the feast as soon as bluebirds return—the best-stocked feeder may get the early birds.

Secret Weapon

Bluebirds love a birdbath as much as they appreciate a feeder—maybe even more, especially when puddles are frozen. Keep yours brimming with water, and clean it frequently.

Simple Saucers

If spring brings below-freezing temperatures, invest in two inexpensive plant saucers for bluebird baths. That way, it's a quick switch to exchange a frozen one for a fresh one.

Bluebird Recipe

Commercial bluebird foods are popular and convenient, but it's cheaper—and easy!—to make your own. Just scoop out a couple of big globs of peanut butter into a mixing bowl, and then stir in yellow cornmeal to make a dough.

How Much Cornmeal?

That depends on how much peanut butter, and peanut butters vary. So mix as you go—when the dough resembles chocolate chip cookie dough, crumbly but able to form a ball when you squeeze it, you're done.

Extra Special Treat

It's fun to experiment with adding other favored bluebird foods to the mix—fats (melted beef fat or peanut oil are welcomed), chopped nuts, or dried mealworms.

Little Bites, Please

Bluebirds have small, weak bills made for eating insects, not seeds, so keep your offerings to small bites.

Chop It Up

Chopped fresh apples, chopped raisins, and any kind of chopped or ground nuts get gobbled up fast by bluebirds. Once you have the birds coming to your feeder, you can mix these into your peanut putter dough, or serve plain.

Starling Proof

Starlings love all these foods, too. So do Carolina wrens, catbirds, brown thrashers, and others. I'm guessing it's the starlings you want to block (easy guess!), so invest in a "bluebird feeder," a wooden box with an entrance hole only small birds (up to downy woodpecker size) can access.

Simple Salad

Easiest vegetable plants of all to grow? Salad greens, which are ready for picking just a few weeks after you sow the seeds. And you can sow those seeds as soon as the ground thaws!

Late to the Party

I'm embarrassed to admit that I didn't grow—or eat!—fresh spinach until I was well into my 30s. I had no idea fresh spinach tasted so different than the gloppy stuff in cans. But once I tasted it, it's been a must!

Spinach seedling

Great Crunch or Easier Cleaning?

The wrinkled, crinkled leaves of "savoy" spinach sure have a great texture, but they're a pain in the neck to wash clean when rain splashes mud onto them.

Anti-Mud Measures

Mulch the row of spinach—and of any other salad greens—with an inch of grass clippings as soon as the seeds sprout.

Cover Every Bit of Soil

Use your fingers to arrange the mulch between spinach seedlings as well as beside them, to cover as much soil as you can.

An Ounce of Prevention

Ten minutes of fussy mulching now will save you lots of time washing off mud later. Mulch along every row, and between individual plants, and you can eat your greens straight out of the garden without feeling grit against your teeth.

Skip the Iceberg

Planting lettuce? Go for "looseleaf," which you can snip in just a couple of weeks, and "buttercrunch," for loosely packed heads that make a whole salad from one plant.

Cut & Come Again

Plant early, and all salad greens will regrow, giving you at least one more round of picking before they "bolt" (send up flower stalks).

Yum, fresh broccoli!

Beware, Broccoli Lovers—SPOILER AHEAD!

I happily ate homegrown broccoli...until I learned how much European cabbage white butterflies like it.

Yuck, fresh broccoli worms :(

Yum, Extra Protein!

Cabbage whites lay their eggs on the plants, and those eggs hatch into green caterpillars that are so well disguised you may never see them until you lift that broccoli floret on your fork.

No Admittance!

The solution? Just cover your plants with a "floating row cover"—an inexpensive polyester fabric you can snug down around the plants to keep cabbage butterflies off. What a relief to enjoy homegrown goodness without getting grossed out!

Kale & Collards

Much easier to spot the well-camouflaged green "worms" on these plants than in a head of broccoli, but who wants to worry about having missed one? Tuck them under those spun-poly row covers, too.

Landlubber Shorebird

One of the earliest migrants to arrive, killdeers are classed as shorebirds, and they do hang out on shores—and also on lawns, parking lots, and other open areas.

Check the Necklace

Shorebirds are notoriously difficult to identify, but killdeers are a cinch—they're the only shorebird with a double-strand "necklace." Look for those two bold black stripes, and you can say "Killdeer!" with confidence.

Double 'necklace' = Killdeer

Where'd That *R* Come From?

The name "killdeer" has nothing to do with the demise of Bambi—it used to be "kill-dee," until somewhere along the line, the final R was added. And *kill-deeee* is exactly what a killdeer says, in a high, shrill tone.

You Call That a Nest?!

Killdeers scrape out a shallow depression in gravel or stony soil, so their eggs don't roll away, and call it good. No twigs, no soft lining, just stones, among which their mottled eggs are perfectly camouflaged.

No Bird Here, Nope

Many killdeers nest right on the shoulder of roads. When the bird is sitting motionless on her eggs, you can drive by within a few feet and never spot her.

Ohh, My Wing! My Wing Is Broken!

That's the act a female killdeer puts on when a predator—that includes us—gets near the nest. She hurries away in a panic, dragging a wing, shrieking in terror because she knows she's going to get eaten. But it's all an act. She's decoying the dangerous critter into following her, so the predator doesn't ferret out her eggs.

Um…We're Still Watching

Back off until a decoying killdeer stops hollering and fluttering, stand quietly or sit in your car, and chances are she'll "miraculously" recover and circle back to sit on her eggs.

Shorebird Showcase

Identifying shorebirds isn't easy, but seeing them en masse during migration is incredible, whether or not you know their names. Tens of thousands of birds may congregate at prime feeding spots to refuel before they complete their journey.

Worth a Trip

Grays Harbor, WA; Cape May and Delaware Bay; and Cheyenne Bottoms, KS, are just a few of the famed gathering places for shorebirds. Google "shorebird migration viewing" to find one near you. It's an unbelievable experience to see thousands of birds rise in massive flocks that shimmer like moiré silk in the sky.

Ah, That Sun Feels Good!

Cold-blooded turtles need to bask in the sun to warm up their sluggish bodies. Look for them piled on logs in ponds on any sunny day in early spring. As the warming sun's rays penetrate the water, the turtles respond, waking from hibernation to groggily swim up from the cold depths to bask in the rays.

Sunning Turtles

Oh Boy, Blue!

Little blue butterflies—and we're talking tiny, no bigger than an inch of wingspread—are one of my favorite delights of spring.

A Tiny Bit of Blue

The blue is on the topside of the wings, so you don't even notice them when they're perched with wings closed, showing only the cryptically colored undersides. But let one flutter by as I'm strolling the garden or wild places, and, boy, I can't help smiling. So tiny! So blue!

Ah, But Which Bit of Blue?

Tiny blue spring butterflies (and their summer cousins) are so confusing to sort out and ID, that I just resign myself to calling them all "spring blues."

Spring Blues!

With dozens of similar species across the country, it's mighty hard to determine the differences even in a closeup photo. And besides, the spring azure is one of the most common and abundant. "Azure" means blue, so "spring blues" it is!

Stop Fighting!

Bird battles at the feeder increase dramatically in early spring—male hormones are kicking into gear, and they're chasing off competitors.

Even usually placid birds that calmly ate side by side all winter turn feisty. It's just perfectly normal behavior for this time of year.

Year-Round Residents

Get your birdhouses up early! Cavity-nesting birds that are year-round residents—chickadees, nuthatches, titmice, woodpeckers—are early nesters. By the time daffodils are in bloom, they're already raising a family.

Second Chance

Even if you've missed prime time, put those nest boxes up anyway! Early birds may experience nest failures (a dead tree blows down, a predator gets the eggs or babies) and need to start over.

Better Early Than Late

Another reason to nail up those nest boxes, even if you missed the first wave: Some raise more than one brood. And before long, other cavity-nesting migrants will be coming in.

Tickled by Feathers

Got a backyard flock of chickens? A duck pond nearby? Collect all the small feathers you can find, especially curled breast feathers, and corral them in a clean wire suet cage. Early-nesting chickadees and titmice will pull them out to use in the soft lining of their nests.

Hey! Who's Pulling My Hair!

A napping dog often becomes a target for nest-making tufted titmice, who may land right on Rover's back to yank out a beakful of hair for the nest.

Canine Collection

Stray dog hairs between patio pavers gets collected, too, by both titmice and chickadees, as well as later migrants like chipping sparrows.

Set Out the Dog Brush Cleanings

Birds use both longer "guard hairs" and downy undercoat fur, so save your dog brush cleanings for the birds. Just set them in an open space.

What Cheer, Say the Boys…and the Girls!

Only the male sings in most species of birds. Not so with cardinals! Both genders sing their spring joy to the world, whistling their trademark *"What cheer! What cheer! Cheer! Cheer! Cheer!"* and variations.

Chorus Frog on thumbtip

Spring Chorus

I've been a frog lover ever since I can remember, thanks to a small pond near our house where I could listen to singing frogs, see strings of black-dotted frog eggs, and bring home a few tadpoles to raise in jars. Now's the time to attend a concert near you!

Fingertip-Size Frogs

Listening to frogs is easy—just sit by still water in spring—but seeing the singers is surprisingly hard,. Some of the loudest singers are the tiniest species: We're talking barely fingertip size for spring peepers and chorus frogs.

Spotting the Singers

Leisurely scan the water and vegetation while you watch for movement, which is likely to be the throat sac of a frog inflating and deflating as it pumps air in to sing.

Second One, A Little Easier

Once you spot your first spring peeper or chorus frog, the next one is a little easier—but not much. These tiny guys are adept at hiding among vegetation in and around the pond.

Patience Pays Off

Being patient is one of the hardest challenges for me, but it's a must when you look for singing frogs. Settle yourself in a comfy spot at the edge of a spring pool or pond, and just wait. I know, I know, it's hard!

How Long, Oh, How Long?

Figure on at least 10 minutes before you spot your first singer in a pond or watery ditch that's throbbing with the spring chorus. Could be shorter, though, if you get lucky!

Who's Running a Finger Down a Comb?

Itty-bitty chorus frogs, of course! And, boy, are they fun to imitate, by making that same sound in the back of your throat—an *"uh-uh-uh-uh"* in a rising trill, the same sound as when you run your finger down a plastic pocket comb.

Kids Love Frogs

Take a little kid with you when you go to a chorus frog pond. They're great at making the sound...and at spotting the singers!

Spring Peepers

Turn It Up!

When a zillion chorus frogs or spring peepers (okay, maybe 50 or 100) are singing at once, the sound is deafening. Cup your ears to bring it in at maximum volume for a few seconds—it's incredible!

Post-It Notes

Keep an eye on the tops of fenceposts next time you take a springtime drive in the country—that's a favored perch for meadowlarks, one of the earliest spring arrivals. And keep your ears open, because that sweet, melancholy song will be repeated over and over.

Shining Like the Sun

Meadowlarks are about the size and shape of starlings, chunky and short-tailed. But, wow, what a front view! Look for that shining yellow chest when the bird is perched on posts, singing its heart out.

That yellow breast shines like a spotlight!
— Meadowlark —

Oh Boy! Vultures Are Back!

An indisputable sign of spring, much more reliable than robins—the return of turkey vultures! Watch for that unmistakable V of their huge dark wings ("V for vulture") as they tilt over roads and fields, looking for a meal.

A Juicy Feast

Robins aren't the only birds who take advantage of good grub in the soil. And "grub" is the word, because that's exactly what those starlings and flickers on your lawn are seeking: not worms, but grubs.

What's a Grub?

Grubs are the plump larvae of Japanese and other beetles, which live in the soil or in dead wood until they're ready to pupate and then emerge as adult beetles.

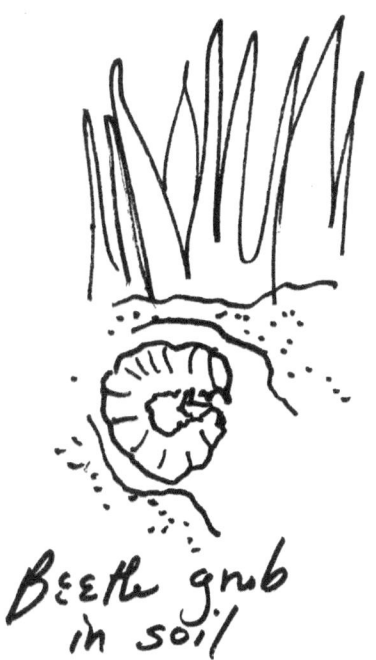

Beetle grub in soil

Moving On Up

Like worms, grubs in the soil also move upward come spring, putting them in easy reach of hungry starlings and flickers.

The Bird We Love to Hate

Is there a more reviled bird than the starling? Well, maybe the English (house) sparrow. Both show up in big numbers at feeders and gobble up way more food than many of us are willing to share.

Portable Pest Control

Next time you're griping about starlings, keep in mind that they're one of the prime predators of Japanese beetles-to-be. Focus your binoculars on a flock on the lawn to catch a glimpse of grubs going down the hatch.

The Ferrari Flowers

Some wildflowers are race cars—zooming into growth when the time is right, blooming in as little as a week after they break ground, maturing and setting seed, then fading away.

"Spring ephemerals" of deciduous woods, and alpine or desert wildflowers, do the whole shebang in as little as six weeks!

One Big Burst

Deciduous forests are home to the best display of spring wildflowers. So are alpine meadows, which are solidly carpeted with bloom. Deserts, ditto.

Hurry, Hurry, Hurry!

Why such a concentrated burst? Time is short! For woodsy wildflowers, it's shade—tree leaves filling in—that ends the season. For alpines, snow; deserts, heat and dryness.

0 to 60 in Just Weeks

The vast majority of the wildflowers in deciduous woods are *spring ephemerals*—plants that hurry into bloom in spring and fade away once the tree leaves fill in. They need sun to make the food for the roots to store for the long sleep that lasts most of the year. Eight weeks of growth and bloom, max—and the rest of the year, sleeping underground.

Speed Demons

Alpine wildflowers are even faster: As little as six weeks between the melt of winter snow and the start of the next season's snow. Desert wildflowers, about the same six weeks as alpines, though some years can be even briefer.

Keep Track of Timing

Most of us don't have a high mountain or desert in our backyard, so we need to take a trip to see the super bloom. Check online to find websites that keep track of the bloom, so you can time that trip. Not much fun to get to Death Valley and discover that you missed it!

Meadow in a Can

Early spring is perfect for planting wildflower seeds, but temptingly packaged "meadow in a can" seeds cost much more than they're worth.

Those cans are chockfull of filler—ground corncobs or the like that supposedly are included to prevent you from sowing the wildflower seeds too closely. I think they're there just to pad out the can, so sellers can make it seem like it contains more seeds than it actually does.

Wind Song

Two of my favorite very early migrants use their wings to make music to woo a mate, rather than their voices. The American woodcock and the common snipe are lookalike species, both short-legged, plump, and dumpy-looking, but, boy, are they glorious in the air when they do their early spring courtship flights!

Field Trip

Neither woodcocks nor snipes are backyard birds, unless you have a damp woods (woodcock) or good-sized pond (snipe), but listen for them next time you visit a wild place in spring.

Room to Maneuver

Both seek an open patch of land to start and end the display, and snipes often perch on posts, too, to sing—with their voice.

Unlikely ∂εralist —
American woodcock

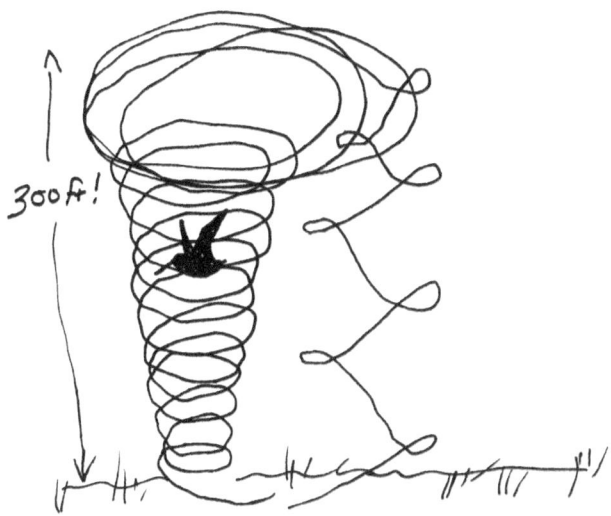

300 ft!

Singing Feathers

Up, up, up, the male woodcock climbs, then suddenly spirals down at top speed, wind singing through its wing feathers. Snipe do a simpler pattern of huge, wide swings.

Wind in the Wings

The sound that goes with these incredible flights? In woodcocks, that's a rapid, musical twittering, in snipe, an unearthly *hoohoohoohoohoohoohoohoohoohoo*.

Cold Blood Craves Sun

Like turtles, frogs, and other cold-blooded critters, snakes are quick to respond to warming soil and sun. Maybe one year I'll remember that....

Aw, I Love Snakes!

I love snakes—as long as I see them first. And that includes even the poisonous ones, which are fascinating to look at and to watch...as long as I see them first.

ACK! I Hate Snakes!

Snakes that take me by surprise? No thanks! They make me jump while my heart races in instant panic. Natural instinctive responses, of course. One wants time to assess danger, rather than have it arrive in a flash.

Soaking Up Spring

Many years ago, when I was exulting in the burgeoning life of the first warm spring day, I sat myself down on a sunny, grassy bank to listen and watch. Best way to notice everything around me.

Spring Day Nightmare

Did I say burgeoning life? Unbeknownst to me, the vibration of my posterior hitting the ground must've been enough to wake the garter snake den I didn't know was beside me.

Suddenly, like in a nightmare, dozens of snakes came boiling up out of a little hole in the ground, slithering away as fast as they could go. Ever since, you bet that I'm way more careful about where I sit in early spring!

The stuff of nightmares!

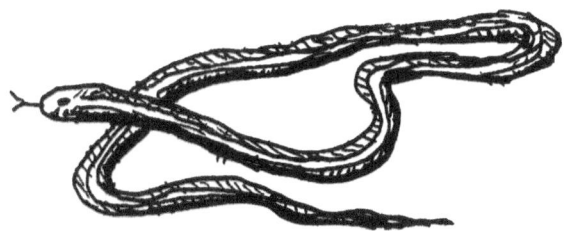

Snakes Are Out!

The first snakes are always out way earlier than I expect, even before the woodsy wildflowers bloom. I'm never even thinking snakes when the first blacksnake—usually a 5-footer!—meanders across my path.

Sideways Stripes

Almost any snake with longitudinal stripes—stripes going the long way along its length—is a safe snake. Note that "almost"! But by far the most common sideways-striped snakes are garter and ribbon snakes, none of which is venomous. No danger, unless you're a mouse or frog or other small critter on the garter snake's menu.

Snakes, in Spades

If you're anywhere near Manitoba in early spring—that'd be May, way up there—check out the Narcisse Snake Dens, about 80 miles from Winnipeg, where you can watch tens of thousands of red-sided garter snakes come alive after hibernation. Me? I think I'll skip it. A few snakes is enough for me.

Screeks and Creaks

The screeching, grating calls of a flock of grackles are an early sign of spring, as these blackbirds, along with their relatives, the red-winged, Brewer's, and rusty blackbirds, move north on migration. Often, a flock will settle for a while in treetops, and when they do, you'll hear them!

Constant Noise

If a flock of grackles settles in your trees or on the ground in your yard, flipping over leaves to search for edible morsels, they'll make enough noise to be heard all over the neighborhood.

Sudden Silence

But wait for the moment of silence—just before they take to the air en masse, every grackle goes silent. Then all you hear is the rush of wings, as the flock moves on.

Homebodies

Nearly all birds with the word "woodpecker" in their name, from that cute little downy to that giant pileated you may be lucky enough to host at a suet block, stay in the same area year-round.

Wandering Woodpecker

Many of the big brown woodpeckers known as flickers stay year round, too, but some do come and go with the seasons, returning in early spring.

Loudmouths

Flickers yell out their name (well, sort of) over and over in early spring, with a ringing "*WHICKA WHICKA WHICKA!*" call.

Flash of White

The name "flicker" may also come from the white patch on the bird's rump, which shows—although it doesn't flicker—as the flicker flies.

Who's That Hollering?

Only the much larger pileated woodpecker has a similar call and volume, so it's worth investigating the source when you hear a bird sounding off—could be a giant Woody Woodpecker lookalike instead of a flicker.

Ants & Flickers

Flickers and ants go together like... love and marriage? horse and carriage? These big birds spend a lot of time on the ground, dabbing up ants with their barbed tongues, or poking at the decaying stumps of trees to uncover a colony full of tasty ant eggs and pupae as well as adults.

Pass the Soap, Please

Flickers even use ants as "soap," wiping their feathers with a clenched beak full of ants.

The smashed ant bodies release formic acid, a natural pesticide that kills feather mites and other insects that may be giving a flicker fits.

Woodpecker "Bathtub"

Where does the flicker bathe with its ant "soap"? Often, right on top of an ant mound.

Snacking and Scrubbing

Sitting on top of an ant home allows a flicker to grab a fresh supply to continue the cleanup. It will ruffle its feathers in the fine grit excavated by the ants...and enjoy ant snacks without even getting up.

Goldenwings

That's what my mom used to call the flickers in our Pennsylvania backyard, thanks to the rich golden yellow undersides of their wing feathers, which flash in flight.

"Redwings"

Flickers sport deep salmon to red-orange underwings in the West, instead of the gold of the Eastern version. Head markings change, too, but it's those colorful wings we notice first.

Middle of the Road

Along about the Great Plains, from Canada to Texas, eastern and western flickers get friendly with each other. They interbreed, creating "intergrade" versions that show elements of each.

Snowdrops

How Early Do You Want Flowers?

Super early. Snow still on ground early. Make your heart sing when winter won't lose its grip early. That's when snowdrops, crocuses, and dwarf *Iris reticulata* burst into bloom! Try 'Harmony', a beautiful bluebird-blue variety of the typical reddish purple dwarf iris.

This Time, Next Year...

I'm so glad to see that bulb sellers are now putting out their catalogs in spring, when the bulbs are blooming and we're all overcome with plant lust! Order when the catalogs arrive, before you forget all about the early bloomers in the big rush of garden flowers that will soon be blooming. Spring-blooming bulbs have to be planted in fall, and suppliers will ship when the time is right.

Good Things, Small Packages

The earliest spring bulbs to bloom are the little guys, so don't just skip past that section of the catalog on your way to daffodils and tulips! Not only are they earlier to bloom than larger bulbs, they're a real bargain as far as price.

Plant by the Dozen

Shop bulk sellers, like Brent & Becky's Bulbs, Van Engelen, and others, and you'll find crocuses, snowdrops, scilla, and dwarf irises for as little as $10–$15 per hundred.

Many in One Hole

Small early-blooming bulbs are easier to plant, too, because you can put a dozen in a single hole for a springtime show that'll stop you in your tracks.

Small Bulbs, Small Holes

Even if you go for a less concentrated display and toss those scillas or crocuses across the lawn to plant in a drift, one by one, you'll only need a hand trowel to scoop out a small 3"-deep hole for each one, instead of a shovel.

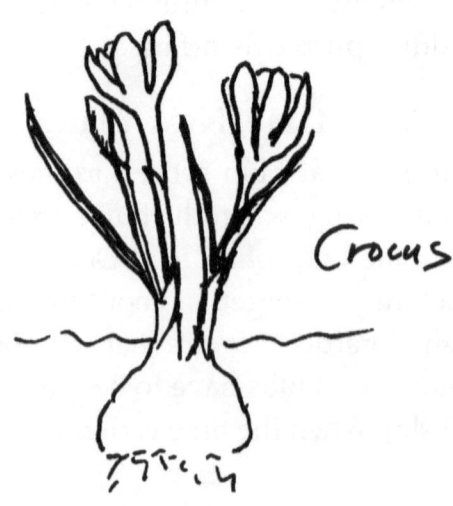

Crocus

Crocuses That Squirrels Don't Eat

Those darn squirrels seem to think we plant crocuses for their dining pleasure. But there's one type that squirrels don't eat. That'd be *Crocus tommasinianus*, or "Tommies" as they're often called, a lovely lavender flower.

A Flock of Tommies

Use sweet little Tommies to create a purple haze across your lawn. Faster than other bulbs to ripen their foliage, they should be done when it's time to mow the lawn. Add more in following years for a wonderfully romantic yard.

Breathtaking Blue

Most shades of blue fade into the background, becoming practically invisible at a distance. But scillas, also called Siberian squill, pack such high voltage electric blue that they stand out as brightly as daffodils.

Scilla
(Siberian squill)

Wildflowers at Home

Short-season wildflowers are great for gardens, because they spring into bloom so early. Who doesn't hunger for early color and flowers, which is what we get from those racehorse "ephemerals" that sprout and bloom in a hurry?

Moving Around

Try species from forests, mountains, and deserts in your own garden. Many adapt easily, no matter where they originally called home. Check the cultural requirements in catalogs and on labels to make sure.

Go for Annuals

Perennials can be fussy about water and soil, but "ephemeral" annuals are simple and successful! Bonus: With the pampering of garden conditions, many bloom much longer than their usual 6 weeks or so in the wild.

Desert to High Mountains

In my Rocky Mountain garden, at 8100′ elevation, annual wildflowers from the Mojave Desert—blue phacelias, California poppies, and others—are among the most reliable things I grow. They self-sow, and their seeds even survive our –25°F cold in winter.

Built-In Food

Most spring ephemeral wildflowers of deciduous forests grow from bulbs, tubers, or corms. Those plump structures are food storage organs.

A Fast Takeoff

Like daffodils, crocuses, and other spring-blooming bulbs, wildflower bulbs are stocked with enough food to sustain the rapid growth and flowers of the following spring. During the brief growing season, the bulb fattens back up fast, as the leaves make food by photosynthesis.

Mom's Folly

My mom was always trying to dig up wildflowers from the woods on our place, and more often then not, she'd slice off the stem before getting to the bulb, even when she went a full shovel depth down. "Boy, these roots are deep!" Sure are—as deep as 12" for a single little spring beauty (*Claytonia*), 15" or more for a dogtooth violet.

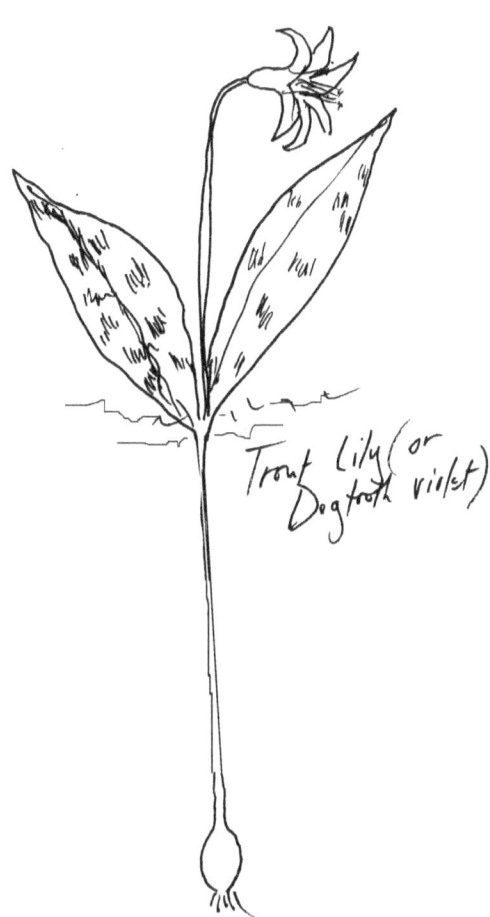

Trout Lily (or Dogtooth violet)

Make Room for New Growth

Cut back the dead tops of ornamental grasses before the new blades start growing. It may look daunting when you're facing a 6-foot-tall clump, but, boy, what a satisfying job, to give the grass a haircut!

No Flat Tops, Please

If you slice off the top of the new growth, your grass will have an odd look all season. Check to see how far up the new shoots are, and cut down the old stuff to just above that height.

Built-In Sandpaper

Grasses of all sorts have minuscule crystals of silica—better known as sand—in their leaves. That's why cutting back ornamental grasses dulls your pruners in a hurry: You're rubbing "sandpaper" against the edge of the blade.

Sharpen As You Go

Keep a whetstone in your pocket to sharpen up your pruners every few minutes, and cutting back those grasses will go much faster!

Make a Pile

Don't shove those dead ornamental grass tops into a trash bag! Lay them on top of your compost pile, or pile a few handfuls in an out of the way spot, shielded from wind, and watch nest-making birds go to town. Birds will gladly take advantage of the easy pickings!

Better Than the Eye Can See

Binoculars aren't just for watching birds outside! Keep a pair by your feeder window, so you can see the details—

how a white-throated sparrow delicately nibbles off the shell of a single tiny round millet seed, how a woodpecker's whole head shudders when it whacks hard at a nut in the shell.

Beware, though—watching your feeder birds with binoculars can make you spend even more time watching the feeder than you usually do!

Color Changers

Goldfinches start to get a blotchy look as spring begins. They're molting into breeding plumage, shedding that dull greenish color of winter and putting on a sunny yellow coat again.

Blotches of yellow & gray? Goldfinch molting for spring!

Before You Shoo Them Away

Starlings change color for spring, too! Take a closer look at those birds that are gobbling up your suet, and you'll see them lose their winter "stars" as they switch to glossy iridescent purple for spring.

You'll Know by the Nose

It's not only feathers that tell the turning of the season—some birds change bill color, too. Starling beaks gradually lighten up from the charcoal gray of winter to springtime yellow.

Male or Female?

Male and female starlings look alike at a glance, but there's a subtle difference to look for: a different color at the base of the beak, where it joins the head.

Pink for Girls, Blue for Boys

Male starlings have a pale blue cast in that area; females lean towards—believe it or not!—a nice girly pink. The colors are strongest in spring.

yellow bill

Starling, spring - summer
No stars, very iridescent

Plant What You Eat

New to vegetable gardening? Start by planting the veggies you love best to eat! Caring for the garden will be a pleasure, not a chore, when there's a harvest of your favorites to look forward to.

Peas & Onions

Those are my favorites for early eating, and I can eat a lot! I've learned a great trick for growing them in quantity: Instead of spacing out each pea seed or onion set along a row, I hoe out a slightly deeper trench (about 4" deep) and dump them in wholesale

Which Way is Up?

My dump-'em-in method violates the rule of planting onion sets root-side-down. Doesn't matter: The growing shoots know which way is up, and they quickly right themselves.

Yes, the white part of the scallion may be curved, but who cares? They still taste great!

Skinny Pea Plants

Pea plants have skinny stems, plus, these legumes make their own food, pulling nitrogen out of the air. So there's no need to worry about them being overcrowded.

Planting Two Deep

Not only can you space pea seeds closely, you can pile them 2 or 3 seeds deep. Just pour them into the trench thickly, and cover well. As long as the plants have a fence to climb, you'll get a yield many times larger than usual.

The Day of Love

Love tomatoes? Of course you do! So make a mental note to connect them with the day of love—Valentine's Day!

Why Valentine's Day?

In many parts of the country, the last spring frost date is about 6 to 8 weeks later. So your tomato starts will be 6 to 8 weeks old—the ideal size for transplanting into your garden patch.

Grow Your Own Starts

Why anybody buys tomato starts at garden centers is beyond me. Oh, sure, I get the convenience factor, but, boy, tomatoes are so easy from seed!

Easy to Grow

Tomato seeds sprout in as little as two days, and grow so fast you can practically see it happen.

Choices Galore

Starting your owl lets you choose from umpteen varieties, instead of only what the garden center has on the rack.

Go Solo

All you need is a container of soil—I use everything from Solo cups to recycled black plastic plant pots—and a packet of seeds. ANY homegrown tomato beats its supermarket kin by a mile!

Be Determined!

Pay attention to the words *determinate* and *indeterminate* when you're choosing a variety of tomato! Determinate varieties ripen all at once; indeterminate keep producing new flowers and fruit until frost.

Plan for Putting Up

If you want tomatoes for canning or freezing, where you spend a day or two sweating in the hot July kitchen for a year's worth of sauces and salsas—buy *determinate* varieties. Their crop ripens all at the same time, so you can chop and steam and fill those storage containers all at once and be done with it.

Tomato seedlings

Keep On Picking

Is there anything worse than planting a determinate variety of cherry tomato, and having to deal with a zillion itty
bitty tomatoes all at once?! Take a word from the wise, and
buy only *indeterminate* cherry tomatoes and tomatoes for
eating fresh or cooking dinner with!

Watch the Wires

Utility wires along roadsides are a favorite perching place
for spring bluebirds and for the small, slim falcon known
as the American kestrel.

One by One, Two by Two

During migration and when they first arrive at their home,
both species of birds sit singly, but soon they pair up and
sit side by side. Once nesting starts, it's back to one bird at
a time.

Falcon House

If your yard adjoins a field, you may be able to entice kes-
trels to a nest box mounted about 15 feet off the ground.
Or maybe you'd rather not—they do eat small birds, as
well as small rodents and insects.

The Elvis Look

Check out a kestrel through binoculars, and you'll see two
bold black sideburns down each side of the head. The mer-
lin, prairie falcon, and peregrine—all spring migrant fal-
cons—go for the Elvis look, too: All have some manner of
sideburns.

Hovering Kestrel

MID-SPRING

Spring doings really start to rev up in mid-spring.

Resident birds are working on nests or raising families, and more migrants are starting to come in. Birds are still eating up a storm at the feeder, and soon, very soon, the first hummingbird will arrive!

By the calendar, mid-spring runs from the end

of March through April, in many regions. Yours may be earlier or later, date-wise, but you'll recognize it when you notice the happenings we'll talk about in this section. First sign that spring is moving along? Daffodils!

Icon of Spring

A bunch of sunny yellow daffodils, in the garden or in a vase, shout spring loud and clear. To get the most out of your daffs, keep a few things in mind when you order new bulbs this spring.

Long-Distance Showoffs

If you want daffodils to show off from a distance, go for full-size varieties in yellow or with an orange center—

they're the colors that carry, and even a handful of bulbs will make a splash.

Miniatures for Special Spots

Keep mini daffs where you can see them up close when you stroll the yard; they get lost from a distance. Or plant them in a large pot that stays outside in winter; they thrive there, too.

Multi Flowers

'Tete a Tete' is one of the most popular mini daffs, for good reason. It bears more than one flower per stem, usually two to three, and that means longer bloom time, not to mention a bigger effect.

Instant Cure for Broken Necks

Spring snow and cold can break the necks of daffs. Prop them up with twiggy sticks—you'll never notice the supports, only the happy daffodil faces.

The Danger of Doubles

Big, fluffy "double daffodils" are particularly prone to broken necks. Even a heavy rain may bow their heads, creasing the stem. Poke twiggy sticks around and in the clump when they're in bud, so those heavy flowers keep standing.

Be the First on Your Block!

Want to beat all your neighbors to the punch with the first daffodils next spring? Order 'Rijnveld's Early Sensation', a classic yellow daff that blooms a full month earlier than any other variety.

A Flood of Robins

There are *a lot* of robins in this country, so you'll see migrating flocks on lawns well into mid-spring. Those that stayed year-round nest early; those that came in later will be a few weeks behind.

Look Close at Robin Flocks

The varied thrush, a robin relative with a slaty back, a deeper orange breast, and a striking black necklace, is a bird of the far west. But it's also a notorious wanderer who may turn up anywhere, migrating right along with robins.

Robin's Egg Blue

Everybody knows that color—the turquoise blue of a robin's egg. Find a whole egg of that color on the ground, or a broken half, and instantly we think "robin"! Not so fast—starling eggs and house finch eggs are also robin's egg blue.

Dandelion Appreciation

We're never going to get rid of them, and I wouldn't want to! Dandelions have huge value as food to all sorts of critters, including us.

Flower First

Groundhogs love to eat dandelion flowers. It's an endearing sight to watch Punxsutawney Phil and his kin pluck a dandelion flower, then sit up, holding the stem delicately in his paws, while he nibbles it from the flower on down.

Icy Curls

Pluck a dandelion flower and, with your thumbnail, carefully split a few inches of the stem lengthwise from the

Every dandelion puff holds about 60-70 seeds

bottom. Fill a clear glass with icy cold water, then stick your dandelion into it. Watch those strips curl right before your eyes!

"Cleans the Blood!"

That's what my father used to say whenever my mom would serve up a bowl of dandelion greens for supper. Sounded good, but for years, I never knew quite what it meant.

Kidney Flush

Dandelions have a strong diuretic effect—they make you pee. A lot. That flushes the kidneys and removes toxins from the blood. Cleans the blood!

Pissenlit

That's "pee the bed" in French, and that's what dandelions are sometimes called in Europe. By now, you know why they got that name. Cleans the blood!

Seeds Galore

Dandelion seed puffs aren't only for blowing to make a wish—they're a vital source of nutrition for migrating goldfinches, native sparrows, buntings, and pine siskins.

The Time Is Right

Or should that be "ripe"? All of these birds move north at the time that dandelions ripen their seeds. It's a feast all along the way, because dandelions are everywhere.

Before Dandelions

What did goldfinches eat before dandelions arrived from Europe, I often wonder? The yellow birds are so drawn to the puffs that it seems everywhere you see dandelions gone to seed, you see goldfinches.

Look Close!

Glance at a field or roadside of dandelions going to seed, and what you notice are the yellow flowers and seed puffs. But down among the stems are likely to be dozens of goldfinches and other small birds, feasting on seeds on the stem and on the ground.

A Cloud of Yellow

Walk through a patch of dandelion flowers and puffs, and you're likely to flush out a flock of goldfinches that were feeding down among the stems. Well, hello there!

"Messy" Dandelions? No—Magic!

Tolerate some dandelions, and you'll bring in more of all these wonderful birds in spring—they even eat seeds from puffs that formed after the flowers were mowed off and left lying on the ground.

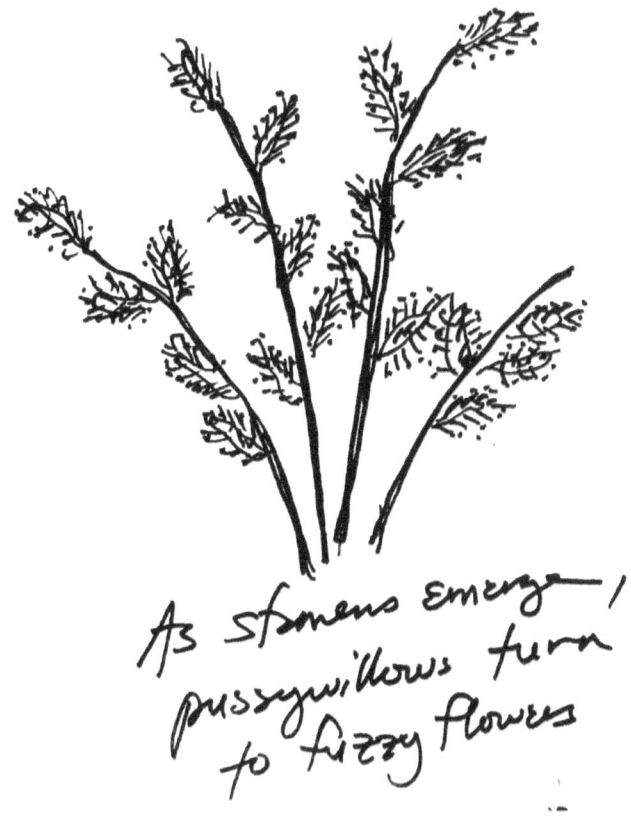

As stamens emerge,
pussywillows turn
to fuzzy flowers

Sharing the Prize

Many times, I've watched a white-crowned sparrow, a goldfinch, and an indigo bunting pulling seeds from different sides of the same dandelion puff. All are mid-spring migrants that eat dandelion seeds along their journey.

Tiny Bird, Big Bite

Tiny pine siskins have a special trick for gobbling dandelion seeds—they pull them from puffs that haven't opened yet.

As soon as the finished, closed-up flower shows soft white fibers at the top, spring-migrating siskins descend, yanking out beakfuls of white fibers—and the seeds attached to their base.

Millet for Buntings

Of course we want brilliant blue buntings at our feeders, too, and here's where millet is worth its weight in gold. Yes, buntings will eat expensive niger, but white proso millet is even more appealing to them—and lots cheaper.

Proso Millet Seedhead.

Small but Mighty

White proso millet is the tiny, round, light tan seed you find in birdseed mixes. And, boy, is it one of the best bargains in birdfeeding, because a little goes a long way.

Multitudes of Seeds

By actual count (thanks, Matt!), at least 600 hundred white proso millet seeds fit in a teaspoon! That's close to *thirty thousand seeds in a cup!* (Black oil sunflowers? 40 per tsp; 1900 per cup.)

Be Sparing

Birds eat the small seeds of millet one by one, and it takes them all day to clean up a small serving. Be sparing, not over-generous—uneaten seeds quickly mold on the ground.

Small Seeds for Small Birds

Mid-spring is boom time for small seed-eating birds at the feeder, and especially millet-eaters. This is when native sparrows migrate, and you're likely to host a mixed batch of 20 to 100 or more if migrating sparrows decide your feeder is a good spot for R&R along the way.

The Sparrows Are Coming!

More than 30 species of native sparrows range over the country, and you're likely to see a good sampling of at least some of them.

Got Any of These?

The most likely spring-arrival sparrows in most regions are migrating song, chipping, and tree sparrows, but other species may show up anywhere along their route.

Start with the Head

Sparrows all look alike at first glance, and lots of bird lovers throw their hands up at the thought of sorting them out. But if you take a good look at their heads, you can narrow down the possibilities quickly. Some have caps, some eyestripes; some, differently colored beaks.

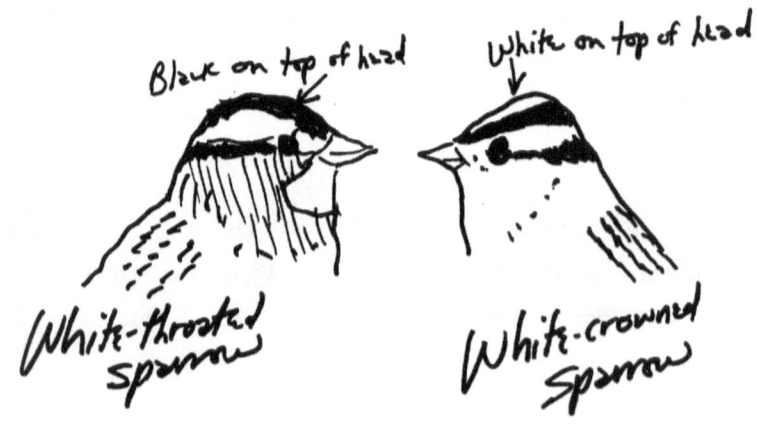

Memory Aid

I learned just how bad my memory was for details when I was learning to ID sparrows! I'd think I had all the details fixed in mind, then open the field guide and realize, um, no.... So snap a pic or draw a quick sketch, to help you remember what you saw.

Check the Stickpin

Look at the breast of the sparrows you're trying to sort out—some have a "stickpin," a dark spot on the breast that helps narrow it down.

"Spot" a Tree Sparrow

Tree sparrows and field sparrows look a lot alike—but tree sparrows have a breast spot that field sparrows do not.

Sparrows of a Different Sort

Lots of folks shudder at the word "sparrow," envisioning a noisy flock of house or English sparrows, the non-native birds that swarm feeders year-round. They're an entirely different animal than our native little brown birds—the sparrows we want to attract.

Bargain Banquet

House sparrows will eat millet, but they're even fonder of cheap chick scratch or cracked corn. Not so the native birds—millet is their prime target, and they only eat the other foods as a last resort.

Decoy Feeding

Spread chick scratch or cracked corn on the ground, in a spot that's away from your feeders, to draw your gang of house sparrows to their own feeding area.

Ground Feeders

Like the winter juncos in your yard, native sparrows prefer to feed on the ground. They'll use open tray feeders, too, but tube feeders don't usually tempt them.

Safety in Numbers

When migrating sparrows arrive in your yard, you'll know it—they move in numbers, usually at least a dozen birds. Often a flock numbers in the scores. Sometimes you'll see hundreds traveling together.

A Foxy Loner

Of course we need an exception to the rule of sparrows flocking together, and that'd be the big, heavily streaked fox sparrow, who often arrives alone at a feeding station.

Look for the rusty red version of this species in the East and Midwest; in the West and Northwest, Foxy is usually dark brown.

Migrating in a Mix

Various species of native sparrows flock together while they move. Safety in numbers, and fun for us birdwatchers, to see how many species we can ID in the batch.

The More, The Merrier!

Native sparrows like to have company while they eat, too. They'll happily peck at seeds just a few inches from each other when they make a refueling stop at your feeder.

Use the Ground as a Feeder

A tray feeder accommodates a bunch of sparrows, but scattering seed right on the ground gives a crowd even more room to gather. With millet costing only about $15–$20 for 50 pounds, you don't have to worry about wasting expensive seed.

Bolstering the Population

Spring sparrows join their winter-resident kin at feeders, the white-throated and white-crowned sparrows that have livened up the feeder scene all winter.

More Millet!

Another good reason to stock up on millet for sparrow season! Winter sparrows don't depart until late spring.

Grow Your Own

Agile little sparrows often cling to grass or weed stems to pluck off seeds. Grow a living "bird feeder"—a garden of seeds on the stem for months of fun watching. Just sow a patch or row of those millet seeds; they grow as fast as grass, because that's what millet is.

Plain & Fancy

White proso millet is the least expensive of the various millets sold as birdseed, and it's the most beloved by birds. But if your budget allows, feel free to experiment with red millet, pearl millet, or even those long sprays of "finger millet" sold for cage birds.

Seedlings En Masse

Lots of seeds get spilled beneath feeders, and lots of those seeds sprout. I let them grow, even though they're crowded together, because many will manage to get big enough to bloom—and birds love sunflowers, safflowers, and millet on the stem.

Sunflower Seedling

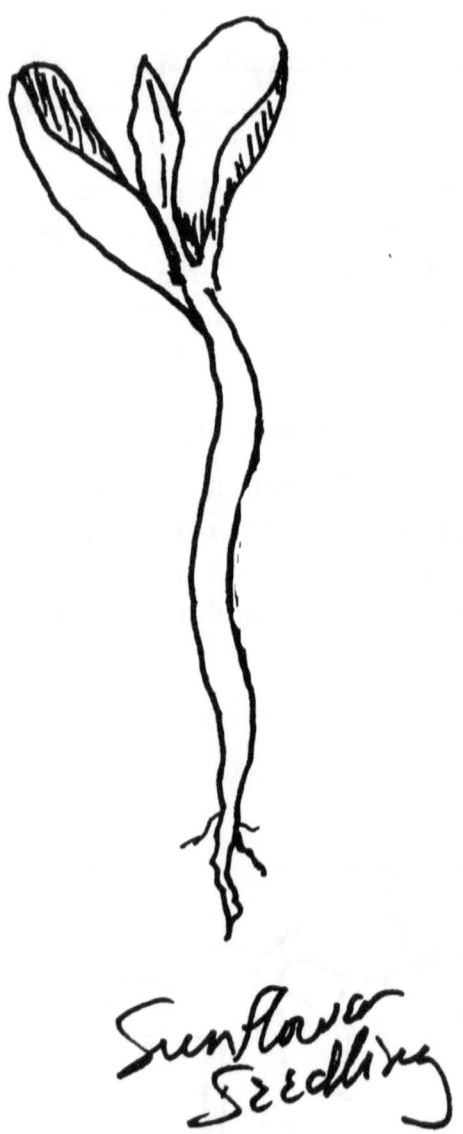

Sunflower Seedling

Eat Your Sprouts!

Sunflower sprouts are yummy! When I pull strays out of my gardens (not beneath the feeder, where bird droppings accumulate!), I eat the whole thing, right down to the roots.

Gardener Jays

Jays have a job—to plant seeds. They're actually *caching* food for lean times, but many of those seeds never get collected.

Gardener Jays

In spring, the seeds buried by jays sprout into oaks (from buried acorns), pines, and pecans and other nuts (from any nut in the shell). Carefully pull up a tree sprout, and you'll see the nut or acorn still attached!

Peanut Plantation

When I lived in lived in mild Zone 8 in Washington state, I found unusual plants popping up all over my gardens—a yellow-flowered legume that wasn't in my field guides. Turned out to be peanuts, planted by jays!

Where'd Those Sunflowers Come From?

If you have jays at your feeder—and who doesn't?— you're apt to find little clusters of sunflowers sprouting in your gardens. Thank the jays, who took the seeds under rocks or in other niches.

Make a Silk Purse Out of...

A metaphorical sow's ear—that wet spot that goes squish, squish, when you walk on it. It's not unusual to have a low spot in the yard where water takes forever (okay, maybe a week or two) to go away, especially in clay soil. Why fight it? Make it a wet garden!

Plant Those Pussywillows!

That vase of pussywillow clippings you coaxed into bloom a month ago are an ideal start for your soggy-bottom garden—they already have roots, and willows love wet feet! Dig a hole, stick them in, firm up the soil, and they'll start sucking up that extra water soon.

No Skunk Cabbage, You Say?

Darn! I was just going to recommend it for that wet spot. Okay, then, how about fabulous, spectacular, drop-dead-gorgeous—how may adjectives can I throw in?—Japanese irises (*Iris ensata*) with their huge butterflied blooms?

Worth the Price

Japanese irises are pricey, because they're much slower to multiply than other irises, and they're prized by collectors, who eagerly await new colors. Expect to pay about $20. These gorgeous flowers are worth every penny—and they'll thrive in a soggy spot.

Fiddleheads

Fern Garden

Transform your wet problem spot into a fern grotto. Plant ostrich fern or cinnamon fern at the edges of your wet spot; royal fern, right where the water collects.

Fiddlehead Season

All ferns arise in spring as charming, tightly curled "fiddleheads," but not all fiddleheads are yummy—and some are so unpalatable, they'll make you spit them right out.

A Word to the Wise

Don't experiment with just any fern—some can cause an upset tummy, and several need special treatment due to toxins in the plants.

Tasty Trio

Wild foragers often gather fiddleheads from ostrich fern (*Matteuccia struthiopteris*), lady fern (*Athyrium filix-femina*), and western sword fern (*Polystichum munitum*). Be sure you know your ferns before you try a taste test yourself!

Chickadee Collectors

Afraid to experiment with fiddleheads? Me too, except for a tentative nibble. So I just let them uncurl into fronds that I—and my chickadees—can appreciate. Chickadees collect the fuzz on the stems to soften their nests.

Birdhouses for Migrants

You already have your birdhouses up for year-round chickadees, titmice, nuthatches, and woodpeckers—now it's time to add nest boxes ASAP for spring migrants that will soon be moving in.

Wrens Return!

What a happy day it is when we wake up to the waterfall of song from a newly arrived house wren! One of the easiest birds to entice into using a birdhouse, these quick brown birds are unafraid of us big scary humans.

Wren Engineers

House wrens use twigs and stiff dead stems to build their nests—lots of twigs and stems. Take some time to sit and watch the process—it's amazing to see how the wren pair manages to maneuver those things into the hole!

Garden Helper

Trying to decide where to put that wren house? Mount it on a 4' post right in your garden, and the busy birds will gobble down aphids, caterpillars, and other garden pests for months!

House Wren

Big Flycatchers

The spring soundtrack changes when big, noisy great crested flycatchers (and their western counterpart, the ash-throated) return and begin courting. These cavity nesters will quickly adopt a nest box as a reasonable facsimile of that natural hole in a dead branch.

Reduce Your Blood Pressure

House (English) sparrows will take over bluebird boxes. If you've been frustrated by this in the past (and it is *super* frustrating!), or if you're new to bluebird boxes, consider feeding-only, instead of providing housing.

Not in My Backyard

Sparrows taking over your bluebird boxes? Find an amenable landowner in the country, where house sparrows are less likely to seek homes, and ask if you can put up bluebird boxes on their place.

Mi Casa, Su Casa

Robins and house finches have learned to use our porches and potted plants as nest sites. Even with all of our comings and goings, these birds may build a nest over a door or window (robins), or in a hanging basket (house finches).

A Rainbow of House Finches

Well, one section of the rainbow, anyhow—male house finches may be the usual strawberry red, or orange, or even golden yellow. Females are always streaky brown.

Hollywood Finches

Formerly known as "California linnets," house finches are native to the far west. Blame the popularity of cage birds in the 1950s for their vastly expanded range—pet shop owners, who sold them as "Hollywood finches," released their stock when it became illegal to sell them. Today their progeny covers the whole country.

Blue Spruces as Stepping Stones

House finches would have had a hard time spreading across the Great Plains were it not for another fad of the '50s—blue spruces.

Making Up for the Lack of Trees

The dense blue spruces, planted in many front yards, provided shelter and nest sites to house finches—something that was lacking in the vast open spaces of the Plains.

Family Time

White mid-spring nesters are busy pairing up, earlier birds are already raising families. Listen for the loud voices of baby woodpeckers. You'll hear them from across the yard—or from half a block away!

No Such Thing as "Bad Birds"

There are annoying birds. Frustrating birds. Big-eater birds. But there's no such thing as a bad bird—that's a label we humans slap onto species whose behavior we find offensive. Every bird has its place in the wild world, whether we like it or not.

Bison Birds

Before European settlers arrived, cowbirds followed the bison that once roamed much of the country, plucking off ticks and other insects on the big animals.

Cow Birds

Once cattle arrived, cowbirds kept doing the same. You can still see them performing this valuable service in farm pastures and on bison in national parks.

Shirking Parenthood

Raising a batch of nestlings is hard work. Hundreds of trips a day to stuff food down those gaping beaks, whew, avoiding the work of parenting. Cowbirds lay their eggs in other birds' nests—a big reason we love to despise them.

It's Our Fault

Part of the reason for the drastic decline in the population of many birds—especially forest birds, such as wood thrushes—is because of cowbirds. That's our fault. We carved up the forests for homes and farms and built roads through them, giving cowbirds easy access.

And Now We're Watching

Back before the boom in birdfeeding, cowbirds went about their business barely noticed. But now we're paying atten-

tion to the birds in our yards, and seeing a pair of cardinals tending a fledgling cowbird makes us mad.

What Can We Do?

Not much, other than hope birds smarten up—and they
are! Some have learned to recognize cowbird eggs and toss
them overboard.

Second-Story Nest

Other cowbird targets, including the yellow warbler, add
on to their nest, building over the top of the cowbird egg
and laying a new set of their own.

Don't Worry, Be Happy

Meanwhile, have a listen to those cowbirds at the feeder,
without fuming. Their liquid songs are among the most
beautiful of spring singers.

Everywhere There's Water

Mid-spring is prime time for migrating ducks. No lake in
your backyard? Just watch for them on ponds, puddles,
and, yes, those lakes, when you take a drive anywhere.

Black Blobs

Ducks don't look very exciting from a distance—a bunch
of dark blobs on the water. Boy, will you change your tune
as soon as you look at them through binoculars!

Best Time of Year

Spring ducks are in full glory, with vivid colors and perfect plumage. And the variety can be incredible, even on a
puddle in a field. Dozens of species, each with its own
beautiful colors.

Temporary "Ponds"

Spring rains bring big puddles to farm fields, and almost every puddle holds some ducks at migration time. Check 'em out with binocs and see what kinds you find!

Go Small

A spotting scope magnifies far-away ducks, but if all you have is binoculars, like we do, peer at migrating ducks on ponds—they're much closer than those way out on lakes.

Habit-Forming

Once you find out that those unexciting black blobs are green-wing teal, blue-wing teal, cinnamon teal, wood ducks, hooded mergansers, stunning shovelers, or adorable ruddy ducks with uptilted tails and baby-blue bills, you're likely to be hooked on a new spring habit!

The white crescent moon on a blue-winged teal's face is a dead giveaway!

Surprise Ducks

Carry your binoculars along in the car in spring, so you're ready in an instant to look at ducks—they can show up anywhere in spring, and that's part of the fun!

"What's This?"

Tree flowers mystify a lot of folks, because many of us don't even realize they bloom. No, we're not talking about flowering crabs or dogwoods, but all of the many trees most of us never think of as having flowers—cottonwoods, oaks, sassafras, sweet gum, walnuts, hickories, ash, and on and on.

Out of Sight, Out of Mind

All trees produce flowers. Trouble is, most aren't brightly colored, plus they're too high to see—unless we make a habit of looking up.

Boy or Girl?

Nearly all trees of this sort produce male flowers and female flowers, and boy, do they look different! So different, that you'll think they came from different trees.

Sweet Gum
Male Flower

Sweet Gum
Female Flower

Pollen Cloud

Male tree flowers have an overload of pollen, to make sure some of it gets to the female flowers. These flowers don't bribe bees with nectar—they rely on the wind to carry the pollen to the female flowers.

Gum Balls in the Making

Female flowers turn into the nuts or seedpods of the tree, and on sweet gums, you can tell right away which flowers are the girls—they're the soft green version of those hard, prickly brown "gumballs."

Look Down!

Make a habit of looking down, because that's where tree flowers are easier to see—on sidewalk, street, or ground, where the flowers drop when their job of pollination is finished, and they give way to the acorns or nuts or other sorts of seeds that follow.

Look Up!

When you find an odd-looking sprig of tree flowers on the ground, look up! The parent plant of those flowers is usually right above your head.

Look Down *and* Look Up!

Connecting flower to tree gives me a whole new appreciation for the trees we often take for granted. Besides, it's fun—and quite the *"Aha!"* moment when I finally put two and two together.

Perfect Timing

Oaks of every kind produce dangling catkin flowers. They're about a month later to bloom than maples, and two months later than willows.

Food Galore

The timing of oak bloom is perfect—just when oak trees are loaded with zillions of hanging, pollen-laden catkins, migrating wood warblers move through on spring migration. The little birds make a beeline for those catkins. Why? Food, and lots of it.

Mobs on the Move

Wood warblers—about 50 species across the country, which move north in mixed-species flocks—follow the bloom of oaks all along their way, starting at takeoff in the Andes.

It's All About Food

Why wood warblers and oaks? They're after any tiny insects they can find on the catkins—and some eat the oak flowers themselves! Pollen is protein, and protein is good food.

Change the Clock

A banquet of oak catkins, just when little long-distance birds need it most: Now that's impeccable timing! Or it was—thanks to climate change, the catkins are blooming earlier. Birds are trying to adjust.

Punctuation Butterflies

By mid-spring, two similar orangey-brown butterflies with scalloped wing edges are out and about. Meet the comma and the questionmark, named for the white marking on the backside of each hindwing.

A Little Wite-Out®

The comma butterfly has a perfect white comma that looks like it was painted on with Wite-Out® on a very thin brush. No such perfect penmanship on the questionmark—you'll need to use a bit of imagination for the top part, although the dot below it is perfect!

Comma Butterfly

Wildflower Bonanza

Warming weather, which creates warming soil, brings a burst of woodland wildflowers.

Go Shopping!

Now's the time to shop for your favorites to add to your shady garden. Thanks to the booming popularity of native plants, you'll find all sorts in native plant nurseries and catalogs.

Take a Walk in the Woods

So many beautiful woodland wildflowers! And catalog pictures can't compare to seeing them in person. Take a walk in the woods and fall in love—you'll feel alive after a spring day outside, and you'll have a hard time holding onto your wallet when you go back to those catalogs.

Same Family, But No Stink

The skunk cabbage of early spring, not exactly a favorite wildflower for most folks, is cousin to a mid-spring bloomer that everybody loves—Jack-in-the-pulpit. Both are in the Arum family, just like the calla lilies of a bridal bouquet.

Preaching to the Choir

Lift that pretty, usually striped hood of a Jack-in-the-pulpit and you'll find little Jack standing in his pulpit. Ferret out Jack's plant for your own shade garden with an online search or at a native plant nursery.

From Shy to Showoff

Come fall, Jack undergoes quite a personality change. Instead of shyly hiding under that flap, he matures into a big

Jack-in-the-pulpit

cluster of gleaming berries that show off bigtime as the rest of the plant dies away.

Centuries of Flowers

Keep in mind, Mother Nature has spent centuries growing that incredible garden we see when we stroll a spring woods in the East or Midwest, or venture to high mountains or deserts for the blooming season.

Reasonable Facsimile

Impossible to replicate in a garden—but we can create a reasonable facsimile. Just plant wildflowers that spread fast, interspersed with slowpokes that take years to make a big mass.

Fast at Multiplication

If you're wanting a pretty patch of spring wildflowers in your yard under your trees—and who doesn't?—start with those that multiply the fastest.

Spreaders

Spring beauties (*Claytonia*) and blue-eyed Mary (*Collinsia*), an annual, throw abundant seed. Bloodroot and wild ginger spread pretty fast, too, as do beautiful blue Virginia bluebells.

Easy Accents

Spring-blooming wildflowers that are much slower to spread make great accents among the larger sweeps of fast spreaders.

Try Jack-in-the-pulpit, trilliums, and hepatica in your shady spots—although they're slow to multiply, they're as easy to grow as daffodils.

What's Cooking?

If you like the smell of ginger in your kitchen, then you'll love the smell of wild ginger in your garden! All parts of the ground-hugging plants are scented. The European type has glossy leaves; the natives, matte.

Oddball Flowers

Lift a leaf of wild ginger to find the weird brownish-red "tailed" flower, which attracts small pollinating flies.

Color, Not Scent

No need to worry about dead-meat smell—it's only the color of those oddball blossoms that call to flies. All you'll smell, should you step on a straggler plant or rub a leaf, is the clean, sharp scent of ginger.

Sally's Choice

Choosing a favorite wildflower is impossible—my choice changes as every species comes into bloom, because I love them all.

Blue Duo

Okay, okay, I'll narrow it down—which spring wildflowers show off best in our gardens? Wild phlox (*Phlox divaricata* and *P. stolonifera*) are a must—billows of soft blue among the daffs and later tulips, because these plants bloom for 2 months straight...and they spread. Virginia bluebells, ditto.

After that, it's up to you! Have fun!

Red-Letter Day

Oh boy, the first hummingbirds! Have your feeder ready and waiting, or you're likely to see last year's birds hovering where it used to hang.

Track the Flight

Thanks to the Net, we can now keep track of exactly how far along hummingbirds are on their spring migration. Go to www.hummingbirds.net/map.html to see how close they're getting to your home.

Ruby-throated Only

That map is for ruby-throated hummers only; if you live in the West, outside of rubythroat range, you'll have to wing it. Mark the first one of your species on your calendar, so you know when to look for them next year.

Special Day Indeed!

Our Colorado hummingbird arrival date is easy for me to remember—it's my birthday. Best present ever!

Early Reds

The more red spring flowers in your yard at migration time, the more hummingbirds are likely to spot them and stop. The more spring flowers of any kind in your yard, the longer hummers will stick around to try them all.

Natives Know

What's blooming at the time of hummingbird migration? All of the native flowers they've been following for eons on their way north! Start with those native to your own region, but branch out with those from other areas, too.

Say 'Welcome Back' with red wild columbine

Time Zones

Their bloom times in their native homes may be earlier or later by the calendar, but once they're in your yard, they'll bloom according to the weather, not the date.

A Trio of Early Reds

All of these early blooming American natives grow well in Zones 5–8 along the rubythroat route: wild red columbine, fire pinks (*Silene virginica*), and coralbells.

Spring Shrub Standout

I'm so happy that red flowering currant (*Ribes sanguineum*) has become easier to find online and in nurseries! The prolific red-pink flowers of this early bloomer are the #1 choice of migrating rufous hummers in its native Pacific Northwest. Other species love it just as much.

Flaming into Bloom

Hummers can't resist the siren call of native flame azaleas (*Rhododendron calendulaceum*), which come in every hue you'll see in leaping flames—red-orange, orange, and yellow-orange.

Long Live the Queen

From the bird everybody loves to an insect we fear: Yellowjackets. If you spot a giant-sized yellowjacket in spring, it's a queen—the only survivor of last year's colony.

Mother of Thousands

The queen is the mother of thousands-to-be—she's already inseminated and ready to lay thousands of eggs. But in spring, she makes only a small "brood nest," where she lays a few dozen eggs to start the workers.

Getting Down to Business

Once the worker yellowjackets from that first small nest emerge, they expand the colony (with the queen laying eggs in each cell) into one of those massive nests that you really, really hope isn't in your yard.

Two by Two

As spring deepens, bird behavior changes among the year-round regulars at our feeders: They pair off. Now, instead of a dozen cardinals or a bunch of chickadees, you'll notice they hang out in pairs.

Mated for Life

Swans are famed for having lifelong partners, but so do many other birds in our backyards. Their lives aren't nearly as long as a decade-old pair of swans—many birds last only a year or two before they get eaten.

Live Long and Prosper

The nest site of a pair of cardinals is one way to tell whether yours are newbies or oldtimers. If a pair chooses the exact same climbing rose year after year, at least one of the birds is likely one of the original pair.

Competitive Sport

Not baseball—morel hunting! Glory goes to those who find the first, the biggest, or the most.

Everybody Wins!

Any morel find makes you a winner, because these spring mushrooms are tender and delicious.

Finding your first morel is the hard part!

Training the Brain

Once you find your first morel, the next one is easier, and those thereafter are a cinch to spot. Why? Because our brains quickly learn the pattern to look for.

Autopilot

Once our brains learn to look for the distinctive pattern of a morel against the leaves, those smart neurons go on automatic pilot. So we can simply scan the area instead of peering closely at every bit of ground.

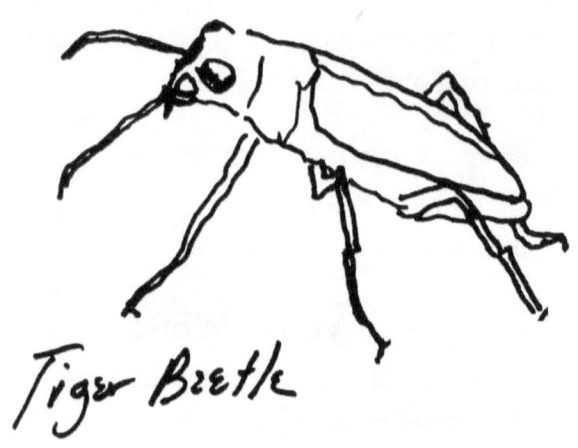

Tiger Beetle

Vicious but Beautiful

As soon as the weather warms, tiger beetles go on the prowl. Incredibly fast runners, these long-legged, solitary beetles are fearsome hunters of insect prey. Various species roam the country, all beautiful, all voracious.

You Won't Even Notice the Spots

One of the most abundant tiger beetles is also one of the most beautiful—the six-spotted tiger that scouts paths and logs in woodsy places and shady backyards from Minnesota to Kentucky and eastward. Forget those tiny spots—what you'll notice is its brilliant metallic color, emerald green, flashing blue and deep purple.

Learn from My Mistake

Don't be tempted to catch a tiger beetle—those big jaws bite! That "Yee-OUCH!" caused me to do exactly what it was supposed to—I dropped the beetle, who ran away lickety-split.

Wearing My Trophy

No, I didn't kill that tiger, but I did find one who'd died a natural death—hard to overlook even a small flash of metallic green when you're out exploring. I wear it in a glass-ball locket, where it flashes its iridescent color like an opal.

Bird-Brained

Male birds are at the mercy of testosterone in spring, and some become insanely obsessed. Their mission is to drive off competitors—and they can't tell a reflection from a real bird.

Battering Birds

Fight! That's the instinct when a male bird at the height of its hormones spies a competitor. And fight it will, attacking the perceived invader with beak, bill, and wings.

Taking It to Extremes

For some hormone-crazed birds, fighting their own reflection in a window, a vehicle mirror, or any other shiny surface doesn't stop when the image disappears. Somehow, they translate that "threat" into the window or vehicle itself, and ever after, it's an enemy.

Recent Regulars

The gray catbird and brown thrasher sure have taken to feeders, now that so many of us are putting out suet and other soft foods. And from the time these migrants arrive in spring, they visit birdbaths daily.

Skip the Bagel

...And just serve the cream cheese. Catbirds and brown thrashers eagerly grab bites off a block of cream cheese in a wire suet cage, because it's a soft food that's high in fat. Buy the full-fat version for birdfeeding.

Kitty in the Corner

Between meals or baths, the catbird returns to shrubby cover, from which it often sings—or mews. Now there's a birdcall *anyone* can ID!

Oh, Go Fly a Kite!

If you haven't flown a kite since you were a kid—or ever!—buy a cheap plastic one in a toy department for as little as two bucks. They're gratifying easy to get airborne.

Reaching the End of Your Rope

Buy an extra roll of kite string, too, because once you have that kite up in the air, you're going to want to see how high it can go. Make sure to attach the new roll before the first roll runs out!

Here, Chick Chick!

Chickens are just as fond of a bite of fresh spring greens as we are, which is how a couple of common garden weeds got their name. White-flowered chickweed and pink-purple henbit are "winter annuals," which sprout in fall but wait until spring to bloom.

Purple Haze

Purple is an Easter color, and purple deadnettle blooms about that time. This is the low-growing European weed that transforms farm fields to great swathes of soft purple.

Give It an Inch...

A winter annual and common garden weed, a clump or two of purple deadnettle is pretty in the garden with pure white candytuft, mini daffs, and other spring bloomers....

And It'll Take a Mile

...Except that purple deadnettle won't stay "a clump or two." Next year, it'll be all over the place.

Back into Bounds

Mints are notorious for overrunning the garden, so bring your super spreaders back into bounds in spring, when the first leaves begin to merge. Uproot straying runners with your hands or a "claw" hand tool; they will pull out easily.

Corral the Mints

Keep your mint patch in a place where you won't need to keep weeding out the runaways. A strip between garage and a concrete or blacktop driveway is perfect, because the paving will stop the spread.

Round Up the Strays

Beebalm or monarda is a mint, and it sure spreads like one! Those traveling underground stems, or *stolons*, are easy to pull up in spring, using only your hands or a trowel, if your patch is crowding its neighbors. Or transplant the neighbor plants instead—a big patch of beebalm is a showstopper!

Spread the Beauty

Transplant those extra beebalm pieces to another area of your garden; they settle in fast. No need to even dig a hole—just push the start firmly against moist soil, and it'll root itself in a few days.

Divide to Multiply

If you've never tried dividing perennials, now's the time to discover how gratifying, and how easy, it is. Wouldn't you love six more clumps of Shasta daisies? Slice up that clump and spread it around; ditto, equally easy Siberian irises and blue catmint (Nepeta).

Tiny 'Armadillos'!

Sowbugs, pillbugs, roly-polies, woodlice, doodlebugs, armadillo bugs—those are just a few of the names for the gray arthropods that roll up tight when disturbed. I've ben calling them "curl-up bugs" since I was a kid, but any name is a good name.

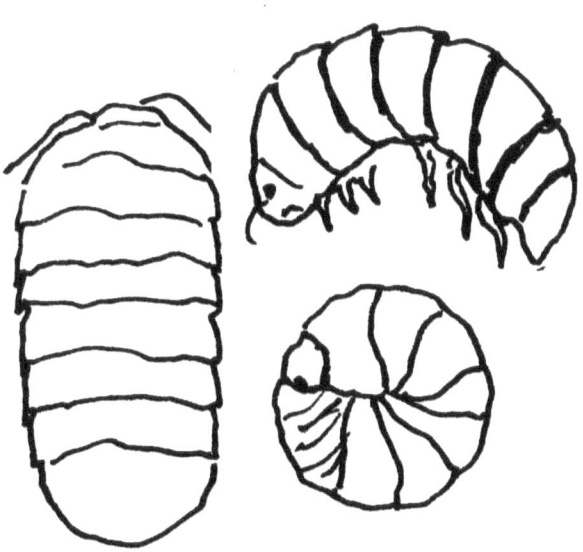

Immigrants and Natives

Curl-up bugs may all look alike to our eyes, but these fascinating critters belong to dozens of different species. Some are natives, but many of the curl-up bugs we see originally came from Europe.

Not Insects

We may call them "bugs," but curl-up bugs/pillbugs/sowbugs/etc., are actually crustaceans, not insects. Look for them in damp, dark places—or when you rake fall leaves off your beds in spring.

"Detrivores"

Now there's a name I'll bet you've never heard! Herbivores eat plants; carnivores eat meat; insectivores eat insects…and detrivores eat detritus—dead leaves and other decaying organic matter.

Living Compost-Makers

Curl-up bugs are one of the reasons dead leaves disappear so fast. These funny critters make compost out of dead plant material, improving the texture of soil.

Many Happy Returns

Self-sowing annuals are an easy—and free!—way to get a lot more color in your garden in following years. All are quick and easy to grow from seed, and all drop hundreds of seeds for next year's display.

Some Like It Cool

Look for packets of these prolific self-sowers, and plant them now—they love cooler weather, and don't mind late frosts or even snows! Try bachelor's-buttons, California poppies, cleome, larkspur, and Shirley (or field) poppies.

Who's Your Mommy?

Self-sown annual seedlings are a cinch to transplant when they first sprout. Learn to recognize which are which, by heeding one big clue: They'll be under and around the parent plant.

Too Much of a Good Thing

Some gardeners steer clear of these plants instead of embracing them—they find the profusion of seedlings an annoyance. If you prefer to have some say in where your flowers are planted, then, yep, give self-sowers a pass.

Sayonara, Seedlings

Easy solution to the "problem" of too many babies? Instead of weeding them out one by one, smother them with mulch.

Kinda Like Capistrano

Swallows are famed for returning on the same date, and around our place, that's the week before my birthday! We often see a few earlier—they're the forerunners of the main flock of migrants, or as some call them, the "scouts."

Swallow Homes

Tree swallows and violet-green swallows quickly adopt nest boxes—and sometimes steal a bluebird house, because the entrance hole and roominess of the box is a good fit for them, too.

Next-Door Neighbors

If a pair of tree or violet-green swallows show interest in your bluebird box, quick, add another house!

Swallows and bluebirds don't mind living near each other. Keep the houses at least 50 feet apart, and both should be happy.

Deeply forked tail?
Barn Swallow!

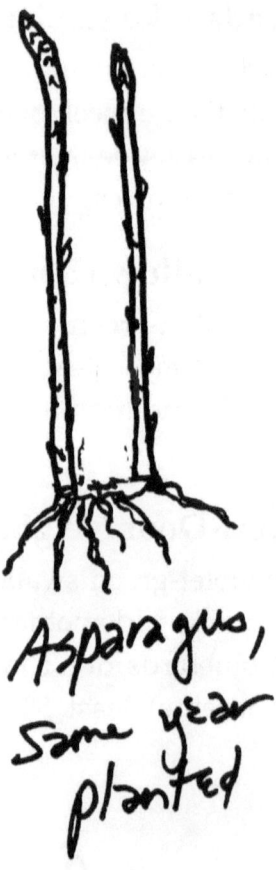

Asparagus,
same year
planted

A Literal Lifetime Supply

Three longtime favorite perennial vegetables can easily
outlive those who planted them! If you don't already have
a patch of asparagus, rhubarb, and horseradish, get going—you'll enjoy them for decades.

Keep It Simple

You'll find all sorts of complicated, labor-intensive direc-
tions for starting an asparagus patch, but I do it the same
way I do every other perennial—dig a hole or row deep
enough to accommodate their roots, put them in, cover
them up, keep them watered.

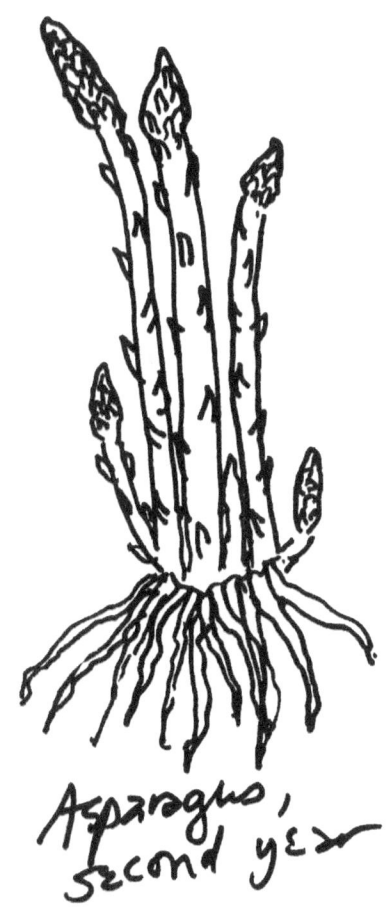

Asparagus, second year

The Hardest Thing about Planting Asparagus

That'd be keeping your hands off until next spring, so the greenery can feed the roots. Bigger roots mean more and bigger spears, so don't be tempted to sample the same year you plant!

Consider Rhubarb a Foliage Plant

The giant ruffly leaves of rhubarb, plus those red stems, are pretty enough to plant a clump in a flower bed—and I do. The bold texture is often just what a flower bed needs to contrast with daintier plants.

Rip Out the Flowers

Yank up that rhubarb bloom stem as soon as you notice it. Flowers drain energy from the plant, slowing down leaf production—and leaves are what we want, for those ruby stems.

Shop the Supermarket

Nurseries and catalogs sell horseradish roots to start your patch, or you can do what I do to save money—buy a couple of roots or chunks of root at the grocery store. Plant them wider end up, and you're good to go!

Fattening Up

Plant horseradish in spring, but wait until fall to dig up some of those spicy roots. The plant needs months of growing for its leaves to multiply and fatten those roots.

Warbler Addiction

Spring wood warblers are nothing short of an addiction for many birdwatchers. So many different kinds! Each beautiful, and all possible in the mixed-species flocks that move through in waves of dozens of individuals.

Count the Kinds

How many species of wood warblers will you see this year? 5, 10, 30? Will you see a cerulean this year? A Blackburnian? A black-throated green? You can play the game every spring at warbler migration time, which runs for about a month, from April to May in many regions.

No Great Shakes at Singing

Despite their name, the voices of wood warblers are nothing to write home about. Most have high, thin, rapid-fire songs that easily get lost in the background symphony of better singers.

Standout Singers

Eventually, you'll get to know the songs of some of the most abundant wood warblers—and the ones who stick around to nest in your neck of the woods.

On Our Way...Elsewhere

Most warbler species are merely moving through, so the only time we get to hear them is when we're watching a wave of the tiny hyperactive birds pass through. But some are summer residents, and their songs become familiar.

"Witchety-witchety-witchety!"

Who's That Masked Man?

Abundant and widespread, the common yellowthroat is a warbler that may choose your backyard for its territory, if you have a lot of cover and a brushy patch, such as a natural meadow garden. Its *"wichety-witchety-witchety"* call is easy to hear—and easy to remember!

Green Doesn't Help

"Vireo" comes from the Latin *virere,* "to be green," and that's the main color of most of these small birds, which migrate about the same time as wood warblers—many of which also are mostly green. Hardly a help in spotting them among the new leaves on trees!

The Preacher Bird

I'm sure whoever dubbed the red-eyed vireo the "preacher bird" wasn't thinking of endless sermons in a stuffy church, nor of strident exhortations. Of course not! Listen for its loud, incessant song, transcribed by Sibley as *"Here I am! Up in the tree! Look up! Up at the top!"* and you can decide for yourself.

Listen, Then Look

Vireo voices are louder than those of most wood warblers, so you can track one down that way first, and then focus in on it with your binoculars to see just who's singing.

checking undersides of leaves for insects

LATE SPRING

If you thought it was challenging keeping up with earlier arrivals, wait'll we hit late spring!

That's boom time for the most colorful migrating birds, with dozens of species of "neotropical migrants" returning from Central and South America.

Mornings are now so full of overlapping singers that it's hard to pick out individual voices. The feeder menu is big on fruit and nectar.

And the garden—well, we're out there every day, admiring the glories…and adding more.

We're talking tulip time here, which is the merry month of May in many regions.

As always, the actual calendar date varies depending on where we live. But birds and plants know what time of the season it is.

Here They Come!

Oh gosh—so many birds to watch for, once "neotropical" migrants from Central and South America start arriving! You'll hear 'em, you'll see 'em, and they're wonderful!

Ohh, The Colors!

Blue grosbeaks! Bright red tanagers! Vivid orange orioles! Okay, I'll stop using so many exclamation points, but, boy, these migrants sure are something to get excited about!

Last but Not Least

Migration starts in early spring and keeps going until late spring, when the last and biggest wave of migration, the neotropical ("New World Tropics") birds, return. That's now, in most areas.

Black, white & stunning red V? Gotta be a rose-breasted grosbeak!

Happy Mother's Day

The first rose-breasted grosbeak I ever saw was at my mom's feeder in Pennsylvania on Mother's Day, around 50 years ago. The most recent rose-breasted grosbeak? At our own feeder in the high Rockies—on Mother's Day last year.

You bet I start looking, wherever I am, on that day.

Big Seeds for Big Beaks

No suet for these big-beaked birds—like their cousin, the cardinal, they like sunflower seeds best. Those strong bills are built for cracking seeds, although, like their relatives, they also have a fondness for fruit.

Tanagers Are Getting the Message, Too

Tanagers eat mostly fruit and insects, but at the feeder they happily scoop up millet seeds. And that's just where you may see these red birds—they've learned that feeders mean easy eats.

Waiting for Leaves

The last wave of migrants, including vivid tanagers and orioles and little green vireos, doesn't move through until leaves are on the trees.

Bringing Up the Rear

That's almost two months after the early travelers, the native sparrows who came through when spring was just getting started. A month behind goldfinches and indigo buntings. But every species has good reason for sticking to its schedule:

Food.

Hey, I like snacks all along the way on road trips, too!

Why So Late?

Birds migrate only when their main food is available all along the route. As spring moves north, so do the birds, because their food is ready.

Meals, Ready to Eat

For robins, it's worms. Sapsuckers, running sap and the tiny insects that come to eat it. Hummingbirds, flowers. Swallows, flying insects. And for orioles and other latecomers, it's insects on tree leaves.

Scarlet Tanager

Insect Explosion

Tender new tree leaves are alive with bugs. We rarely notice them, unless a rain of "honeydew" drips on our cars parked underneath, or a caterpillar dangles from a thread of silk in front of our eyes.

Sharp-Eyed Birds

Most insects on tree leaves are green, for protective camouflage. Watch a tanager or an oriole scouting the leaves, though, and you'll see how intently they peer at both tops and bottoms of leaves. Gotcha!

Add Fruit at the Feeder

Many late spring migrants love fruit as much as insects. It's great fun to experiment with different fruits when these migrants come in, because some of our favorite birds quickly accept it.

Experiment!

Start with the staples—orange halves and grape jelly—but branch out to any soft, sweet fruit or jelly you happen to have on hand.

Good Timing

Late spring migration is the ideal time to serve fruit and jelly, but it's not only because hungry fruit-eating birds are arriving. It's because wasps aren't out and about yet!

Eat and Leave

A feeder feast of fruit doesn't get nearly as much bird attention—or even any at all—after migration is over. By then, most birds have turned to natural foods: insects, and fruit on wild or backyard trees and bushes. Think of fruit as a seasonal treat.

Tropical Fruits for Tropical Birds

Neotropical ("New World Tropics") birds are used to eating all of the many, many fruits in their winter homes—and they recognize them even if that papaya is in a New York feeder instead of on a tree in the South American rainforest.

Everyday Exotic

Bananas are so commonplace that we sometimes forget they're exotic—even more exotic than we think, having originated in Australia and Indonesia.

Familiar to Birds, Too

Bananas have been grown in the Americas for more than 500 years, though. And all neotropical fruit eaters are as familiar with bananas as we are.

Vacation Dining

"Eat like a local" is one of the best things about vacation, whether it's pasta in Tuscany or North Carolina barbecue. Birds do the same—on their wintering grounds, they dine on tropical specialties; on nesting grounds with us, local insects, berries, and fruits.

Eating Out of Season

Consider that dual menu, with feeder offerings—birds may enjoy a taste of that tropical winter home, just as we search for recipes to cook up the dishes we loved best when we get home from vacation.

Easy Access, and Visible

Don't hide your fruit offerings in a tricky feeder—lay them on an open tray instead. That way, birds will see them instantly and not have to figure out how to get at them.

First Oranges in the Americas

Christopher Columbus, 1493. What, not 1492? Not for his connection with oranges—he introduced the citrus fruit, originally from China and India, to the island of Haiti way back in 1493.

Florida Oranges

By 1565, orange groves were thriving in Florida and the trees had even spread to the wild—so successfully that famous American plantsman William Bartram thought they were natives when he came across them in the 1700s.

Opportunistic Eaters

What does all this have to do with orioles? It shows how birds change their habits to take advantage of a bounty of food, whether it's eating oranges...or learning to come to our feeders.

Oranges Are for Orioles

It seems way too neat—that orange-colored orioles love oranges. But it's true. Definitely put out sliced-in-half oranges for your friends, but don't stop there—try other sweet fruits, too.

Orioles love oranges— and bananas!

Always Available

Orange trees don't grow anywhere near our home, nor near many of yours, but oranges are always in our fridge. They're a big favorite for fruit-eating birds who winter where oranges *do* grow.

Orange Is for Orioles?

Okay, now we're going too far, although it sort of makes sense on the face of it: We know that hummingbirds zoom to the color red, so orange plastic feeders for orange-eating orioles make sense to us.

Any Color Will Do!

Just one big problem with those orange feeders: Unlike hummers, orioles lack the instinct to instantly investigate certain colors.

Perches, Please

If you're not a fan of orange plastic décor in your yard, you can use any color of feeder for orioles. Be sure it has perches that will support the birds while they sip or nibble.

Color Clues for Hummers

All native flowers of the Americas that are red (or orange-red, or rich orange) are hummingbird flowers! No wonder the tiny birds zoom to those colors.

The Color Is a Promise

Those colors of native flowers are shaped right, arrayed right for whirring wings, and hold nectar deep in their throats, out of reach of other nectar-drinkers. So hummers have a better chance of getting a meal.

Not Ready Yet

Most fruits are green on the outside before they're ripe—oranges, mangoes, papayas, and lots of others.

Now Ready to Eat!

Once the seeds inside are mature, fruits send a message with color—"We're ripe and sweet now! Eat us!" Birds and animals oblige, and their droppings spread the seeds.

Color Clues for Orioles

Take a look at your fruit bowl, and you'll see you already have colorful fruits. Yellow bananas, orange oranges, rosy

mangoes, yellowish papayas—mmm, you know they're going to be delicious. And so do orioles.

In their Neotropical winter homes, orioles eat papayas + other tropical fruits

Flower Eaters

Same thing with the flowers that orioles seek out in order to drink nectar or eat the blossoms—they're a colorful bunch, from red-hot poker to agave to coral tree, signaling to pollinators from a distance. Orange? Sure, but other colors, too.

Colorblind Test

"Look at that scarlet tanager in the oak!" "Where? Where?" I thought my friend was just having trouble pinpointing the bird, but he had a bigger disadvantage—he was colorblind, and red looked the same as the green leaves to him.

Fast Food Stop

Long-distance migrants stop to refuel just about anywhere there's food, no matter what sort of habitat they usually live in. Food is the main thing on their mind.

Come One, Come All

You may see birds of the forest, fields, desert, marshes— any habitat—in your backyard during migration.

Increase the Appeal

You'll see even more migrating birds, of more kinds, if you have welcoming trees, shrubs, and flowerbeds where they can shelter while checking out the feeder offerings.

Weirdest of All

I thought I was ready for anything to show up—that's a huge part of migration fun!—but I never expected a great blue heron to stand at my tray feeder, shoveling up seeds. Nor did my sister ever expect the black-crowned night heron that came to hers!

Even More Important Than a Feeder

A birdbath draws in more kinds of birds than a feeder alone. Vireos, warblers, thrushes, grosbeaks, orioles, thrashers, tanagers—birds that eat at a feeder, but also birds that don't. They all love water!

Water Music

Announce your tempting water with a trickle, so birds in the area will know it's there. A small solar fountain, set to bubble rather than spray, costs only about $15 but is worth its weight in gold.

Skip the Tip

Easiest way to turn a fountain into a deliciously gurgling bubbler? Just take off the spray tip. The pump will still push water up, but it'll spill over with a gurgle instead of a barely audible spray. Less evaporation; louder invitation.

For Deeper Basins

If your water basin is too deep for the remaining bit of stubby tube on the pump once you remove the spray tip, just buy a length of tubing, of the right diameter to fit over the stub, from any hardware store.

Multi-Level Marketing

Add extra birdbaths in spring—or bird drinking dishes. A typical pedestal bath is a good start, because birds recognize it. Then add plant saucers set about near shrubs, raised a bit on a concrete paver, to give thrushes and ground-level birds easy access to water.

Night Flight

Nearly all migrating birds fly by night, to stay safe from day-flying hawks. Step outside and listen—you can often hear their cheeps and chirps filtering down from the sky.

Some Like It Hot

Your cool-loving annuals and veggies are already up and growing, and now it's safe to sow seeds of annuals and veggies that prefer warm soil.

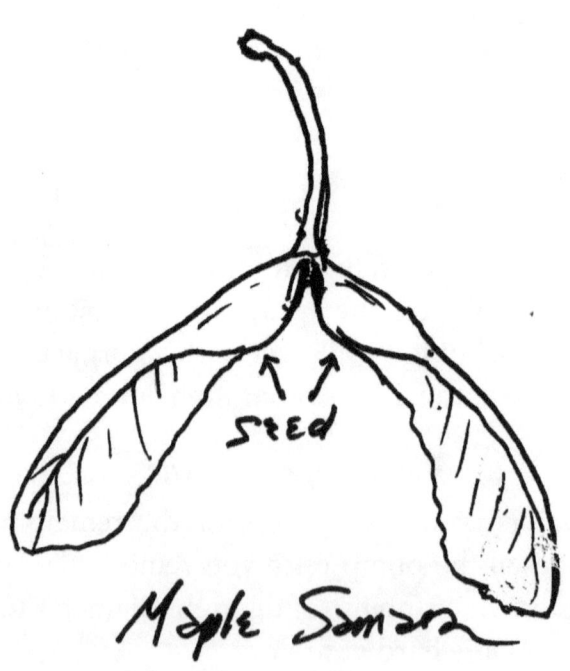

Maple Samara

Easy Annuals

Sow marigolds, zinnias, cosmos, and celosia when you put in your tomatoes, squash, and melons or plant a patch of corn. In cool, moist soil, these seeds may rot, and transplants will sulk.

Whirlybirds

The maple flowers of early spring turn into maple seeds now—the winged seedpods called samaras. When the seeds are ripe, they let loose and helicopter down. Fun to watch the whirlybird flight!

Nosepinchers

We called samaras "nosepinchers" when I was a kid. Snap the seedpod in half, carefully peel the fat end open, and stick it on your nose. Voila! Nosepincher!

What If It Had a Different Name?

I often wonder whether folks would appreciate the common wild daisies called fleabanes (*Erigeron*) if they had a more appealing name? "Dainty Daisies," perhaps, or "Cloud of Spring"? At least we might smile then, when we're weeding extras out of our flowerbeds.

Finest Fluff

Annual and widespread, daisy fleabane (*Erigeron annuus*) goes to puffs of seedheads just when hummers are searching for bits of fluff for their nests. You bet they use it!

Let It Grow

Watching the interactions of birds with plants gives us a new appreciation for even those scorned as weeds. Instead of spending time worrying about keeping your lawn perfect, you may decide you prefer "interesting" instead.

Avoiding Tulip Disappointment

"I don't plant tulips anymore, because they don't come back." Disappointing for sure, but how about trying a few tricks before you give up for good?

Sun Is a Must

Are your tulips in full sun? These bulbs hail from the deserts of Turkey and other hot, dry places, and they need full sun.

Save the Leaves!

Like all bulbs, tulips make food through their leaves to bulk up the bulb for next year's bloom. If you rubber-band the leaves into tidy bundles after bloom, the bulbs get shortchanged. Let them die off naturally.

Short-lived but irresistible — parrot tulip

Give Them Room

Those tulip leaves need sun until they're totally dead. If your tulips are planted among perennials, they may be getting more shade than sun, and that will reduce your chances of flowers next year.

Long-Lived Tulips

Some tulips are famed for blooming year after year. Two early reds keep going for years—short *Tulipa greggii,* a "species" tulip that's the same as it is in the wild, and tall 'Red Emperor', an old-fashioned fave that still can't be beat. Find them in the bulb catalogs that are piling up now.

Three Cheers for 'Toronto'

Salmon-pink 'Toronto' tulips have been a favorite of mine since they were first introduced.

I nabbed them first because of their color—it brightens the late spring garden like nothing else, and it goes with all those early blues and the overlapping bloom of pink daffodils and poet's narcissus.

Multi Flowers

Another reason to try 'Toronto'—each bloom stem has more than one flower! So you get a much longer time of bloom than the usual 10-days-and-done of many varieties.

A Long and Happy Life

'Toronto' keeps blooming year after year, with no special care other than making sure it gets sun. Every year, I tinker with the companions around their feet, but the tulips? They're there to stay.

Change Your Expectations

Instead of getting ticked off when my tulips don't rebloom, I consider it a bonus if they do! Amazing what a difference that can make.

Bye-Bye, Beautifuls

Oh, sure, I shed a few tears when those spectacular parrot tulips, and the amazing 3½ -foot tall whatever-they-weres, petered out so fast. But a dozen bulbs doesn't cost much, and I don't mind investing that money for even a single year's bloom.

Getting Your Money's Worth

Would you still buy a dozen bulbs, knowing they might not flower for more than a few years?

I sure would! Tulips are so beautiful, and such a great big blast of color, that it's impossible to imagine late spring without them.

Violets

Earthly Delights

The garden is as full of delights as the bird world is, this time of year. But you already know that. Enjoy all your friends, look for babies, and...

Go Shopping!

"Plant therapy," I call it, when I head for a nursery or garden center in spring. I always intend to get maybe one or two things...and before I know it, I'm pulling a cart crammed to the brim. Ah well, that's what spring is for!

A Bare Spot!? Where'd That Come From?

If your perennial beds are as crammed as mine, you know how odd it is to find a good-sized empty spot. Three, count 'em, three different years, I've dug into a still-sleeping clump of flowers, trying to fill that precious "bare spot" with something else.

Biding Their Time

Most perennial plants are up and growing early in spring, and many are already in bloom by now. But balloon flower and monkshood are slowpokes. Their first shoots often don't break the ground until tulip time.

Think Before You Dig

That bare spot may be there for a reason. Before you step on the shovel, try to remember what that part of the bed looked like last year. Was there a late sleeper in that spot?

Try Anything!

You never know until you try, so don't be dissuaded by neighbors or experts or gardening books. Come to think of it, don't even ask advice—if you like a plant, give it a try.

Shop an Asian Market

Asian cuisine includes lots of interesting plant parts that most of us don't realize are edible. Buy any root or bulbs, plant it, and see what develops!

Way Cheaper Than a Nursery

Look for fresh, unpeeled *doraji,* the roots of balloon flower (*Platycodon*), at an Asian grocery, and buy extras so you can make *doraji-muchim* (spicy bellflower roots) . . . and plant the rest in your garden.

Young and Dumb

Thank goodness I was too dumb to know better when I bought and planted a pack of delphinium seeds in my very first garden, in Pennsylvania. Big clumps with 6-foot stems of stunning blue flowers? I never doubted that's what I'd get.

Trial and...Success!

My homegrown delphiniums took off. Most of the seeds sprouted, and quickly grew into big leafy clumps the first year, with no special care. And then, the second year—oh my. The towering spikes of blue flowers were even more glorious than I'd ever dreamt.

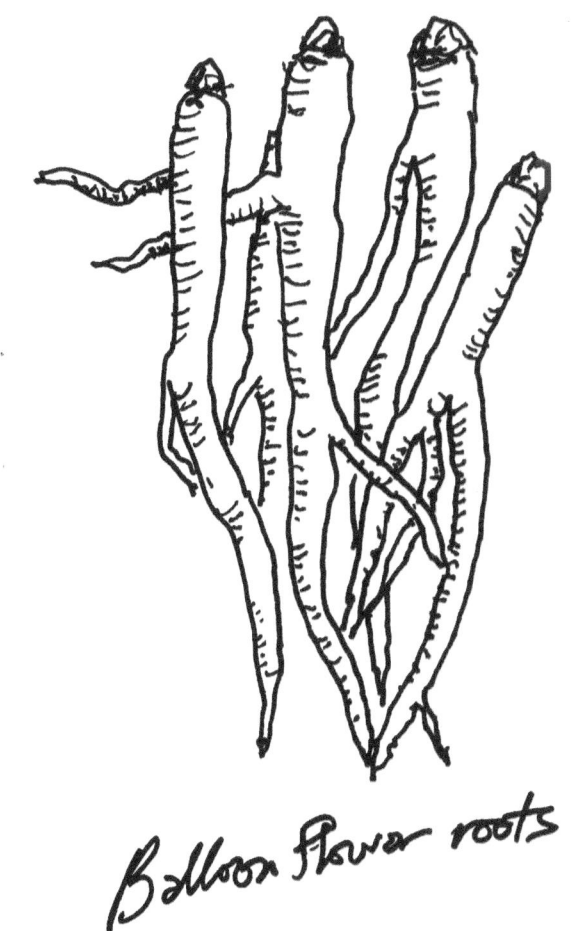

Balloon flower roots

More for the Future

Those delphiniums dropped lots of seeds to start new plants, so the patch just kept growing. Older ones died out, but new ones were rarin' to take their place. Then I read my first garden book…

Oops

"Tall delphiniums only grow well in cool, rainy England and the cool, rainy Pacific Northwest," advised the experts back then.

And, oh yeah, you had to buy expensive potted young plants, certainly not just scatter a packet of seeds. And fertilize them a lot.

Is Pennsylvania Part of England??

I was flabbergasted. I'd done everything wrong, but my delphiniums had turned out great. Ever since, I've been taking "experts" with a hefty grain of salt. Until you try for yourself, you never know.

Wood Ashes for Hummers

Hummingbirds are on home grounds now, and females start looking for "prenatal vitamins." They'll dab up tiny bits of wood ashes for calcium and other minerals.

Spread woodstove or charcoal grill ashes on the ground—female hummingbirds will find them.

Crescendo

At least one morning this spring, make a date for the bird symphony.

Grab your favorite mosquito repellent, and take your seat when dawn is just beginning. Then… listen.

Soak It Up

Doesn't matter whether or not you can name the various "instruments" in the concert—just enjoy the variety and soak up the beauty of the music.

Robin Appreciation

Everyone knows what a robin looks like. But what it sounds like? "Um...I don't know." Change that answer this spring!

Look and Listen

Robins are among the most abundant backyard birds, and their songs are a constant on any early morning. It's melodic and very, um, cheerful—"*Cheerily, cheer up, cheer up, cheerily, cheer up....*" Follow your ears, find the singer, and there you go.

Hatchling Quail

"Precocious Babies"

Wild turkeys, quail, grouse, pheasant, and killdeer babies—all hatching now—are different than those of songbirds. Their eyes are open and they're fully covered in fluff as soon as they break the egg.

Ready to Run

No nurturing in the nest for these birds—once they hatch, it's everybody ready to run, because predators would love to gobble up these tender morsels.

Death Match

Male birds are serious about guarding their territories, and they do occasionally fight to the death. Either combatant—the instigator or the target—may be killed, or sometimes even both birds.

Blind to Danger

When one male bird chases another, neither looks left and right before crossing a road. Road-killed males are common in spring.

Dead Doesn't Matter

Once you start noticing those sad bunches of colorful feathers in the road, you're likely to notice something else—a male bird of the same species still attacking the dead body. These birds often become "collateral" victims, getting hit by a car themselves.

What's Good for the Gander...

...is good for the goose. And in the case of many birds, it's fooling around on the side that takes place by both male and female.

Mated for Life

Yes, many bird species do mate for life—the same pair share the duties of raising a family year after year, until death do them part. But fidelity usually isn't part of that lifelong vow.

Keep Your Genes Out of My Nest!

The eggs in that nest may have a bunch of different daddies—"foreign" males sneak in; females sneak out to the neighbor's. No wonder male birds are so quick to attack!

No Family Heir?

Raising babies is a big investment, and if those eggs are from another male, they won't have the "husband's" genes. No way for him to tell, so he takes preventive action, driving away trespassers.

Wandering Eye

Trouble is, while those chases by male birds are taking place, the female left behind can take advantage of the free time. It's opportunity to host a different male at her home, or take a quick trip to his place.

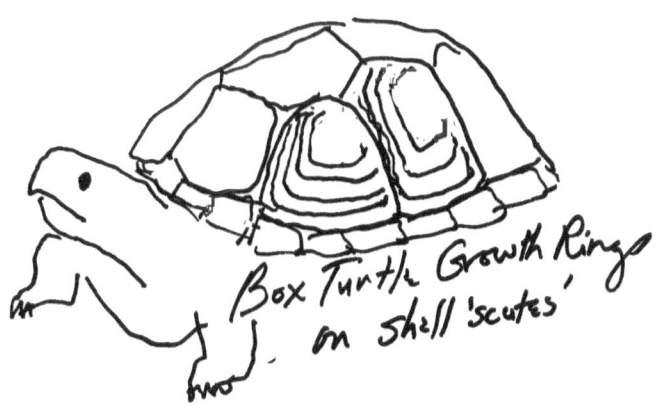

Box Turtle Growth Rings on Shell 'scutes'

Turtles on the Move

Box turtles are super long-lived, 50 years or more, or they were until cars came along. In late spring, like many other turtles, they amble across roads, looking for a mate and, for females, a place to lay eggs.

Helping Hand

Helping a turtle out of danger takes just a minute!

Watch for traffic! Pull over safely, pick up the turtle (unless it's a snapper!), and carry it across the road in the direction it was heading.

Don't Get Wet!

Hold that turtle out at arm's length—peeing is a popular turtle defense. It's harmless, but the surprise could make you drop the turtle on the hard pavement.

Count the Rings?

Folks used to say you could count the ridges on an individual "scute," or plate, of a box turtle's shell to find out how old it is. Nice idea, but not quite true.

Feast or Famine

The ridges form during growth spurts that occur when food is abundant. When leaner times follow, shell growth slows down, leaving the gap between rings.

Reading the Ridges

The high ridges on a turtle scute? Probably spring, when slugs and other foods are plentiful, or maybe summer, when fruit is abundant. The gaps? Might be winter, or a drought, or an unseasonably cold spell in spring—any time that food was hard to come by.

No Way to Know

But box turtles have lots of ridges on their shell, some pronounced, many much slighter. Sorry, but there's just no way to tell age for sure by counting rings.

Transplanting Tomatoes

Tomatoes have a nifty habit of rooting along their stem if it touches the ground. In the garden, additional roots will bring more nutrients and water to the plant, resulting in vigorous growth and great tomatoes.

Bury the Stem

Lay the stem of your transplants sideways when you plant them out, covering it in soil. The leafy top part, left uncovered, will soon right itself and reach for the sun, while the roots that form on the buried stem will pump in extra food and water.

Ouch!

Nothing worse than the thud of a bird hitting the window, and during spring migration, glass can really take a toll. Stop cringing at the thud, and take action.

Which Windows Are Worst?

Most houses have one or two particular windows that birds bang into, with most of the others seeming to be completely out of flight paths. Those too-tempting windows are the ones to focus on.

Collision Insurance

Decals don't help, but turning that deadly pane of glass into a temporary "zebra" will reduce the collisions. Just get some washable white poster paint and paint 3"-wide stripes on the outside of the glass, a few inches apart.

Between the Lines

Yes, it will look funny; no, your view won't be what it used to. But birds will be safer, and, surprisingly, you'll still be able to see a lot of the outside world—you'll look *through* the stripes, just as you do with fence railings.

Toad Song

The American toad usually waits until late spring to start singing, and what a fun song it is! It's a long trill that you can easily imitate.

Trill Like a Toad

Draw back your lips, flutter your tongue, and hum...or something like that. Just try it when you hear toads—your mouth will know how to do it!

Toad tadpoles

Toad at Home

Having a toad move into your garden feels like an honor—and it is. You now have one of the best bug- and slug-eaters around…as well as a friend to say hi to when you spot him/her.

As Sweet as Tupelo Honey

For two weeks in late spring, when tupelo trees (*Nyssa* species) bloom, bees and beekeepers go crazy.

The bees gather as much nectar as they can, turning it into one of the sweetest honeys around.

The beekeepers haul their hives to the trees, so they can bottle some of that legendary sweet stuff later.

Honey in Spring, Flames in Fall

Even if you don't keep bees, tupelo trees are great for the yard. Often called gum trees, these Southeastern natives are total standouts in fall, flaming bright, clear red.

Black or White?

I've never tasted enough tupelo honey to become a connoisseur, but aficionados argue over which is best—that from white gum (*Nyssa ogeche*) or black gum (*Nyssa sylvatica*)? Just pass that bottle—I'll happily eat any kind!

Nosegay Bouquet

Your nose will indeed be happy when you pick a handful of lily-of-the-valley! These old-fashioned flowers (why do I keep using that word so much? Maybe because they're time-tested plants, and I'm old-fashioned myself) deserve a renaissance.

Scented Shade

Tuck a handful of lily-of-the-valley "pips" into your shady garden, and the delirious fragrance will scent the air as you stroll around. Look for them in the same catalogs you shop for tulips and daffs.

Somebody Say "Old-Fashioned"?

Violets are worth a modern audience, too. Dozens of species are native across the country, in all shades of lavender-blue, reddish violet, white, and even pink. Most spread at a moderate to fast pace, flinging seed onto soil and into cracks for springtime charm.

Perfect Pink

"Odorata" means fragrant, and *Viola odorata* 'Rosea' is the sweetly scented, rosy pink violet that stole my heart when I saw it splashed across a friend's spring lawn.

Hardy and Hearty—For Most

'Rosea' sweet violet thrives in Zones 5–9, which is why the sample I brought home from my friend's yard to our Zone 3 garden turned up its toes and died. Search for plants online, or check the Logee's catalog.

Speaking of Pink

Boy, did I luck into a great heirloom when I moved into my first house in Indiana! Years before, the former residents had planted *pink* lily-of-the-valley, and they'd spread all along the shade side of the house!

Don't Get Too Excited

Pink lily-of-the-valley, heavily touted about 30 or so years ago, turned out to be kind of a bust. They're a pale, muddy pink, not a pretty, vibrant color. I shared lots of samples…but I still like the white ones better.

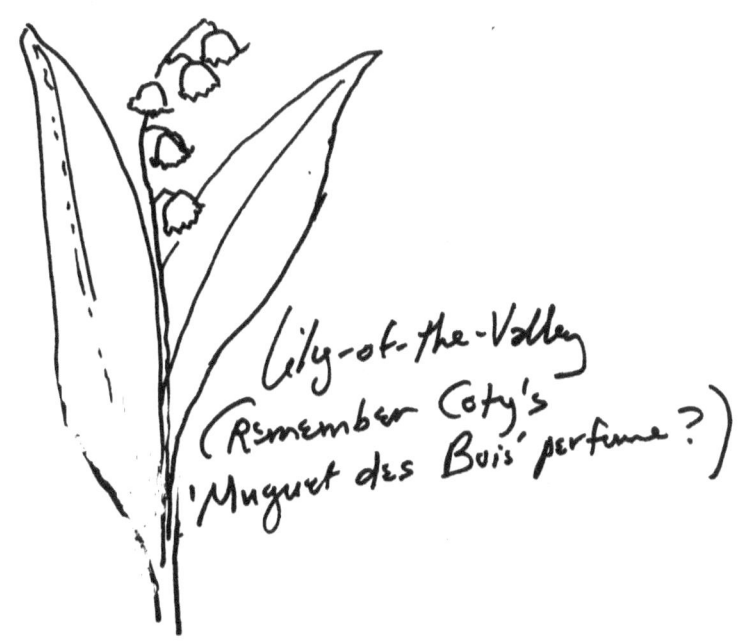

Lily-of-the-Valley
(Remember Coty's
'Muguet des Bois' perfume?)

A Personal Rant

When I hit teenagehood, and wanted to start wearing perfume to wow the boys, I had two excellent scents to pick from—bottled products that smelled like the flowers I love.

They were Coty's "Muguet des Bois," which smelled just like lily-of-the-valley, and Avon's "Honeysuckle," which practically made me swoon. Neither is made anymore: If they were, I'd be doused in them.

Smells Like Clover

If you have clover in your lawn, you'll smell it when you mow the grass. That delicious scent, like new-mown hay, comes from the coumarin in the plant.

Coumarin Gone Bad

When sweet-smelling coumarin is attacked by certain fungi, as can happen in moldy hay, it turns into coumadin, the well-known blood thinner sold as Warfarin.

Cows Gave the Warning

Coumadin is great for blood-clot patients, but bad news for cows that eat it—they can hemorrhage after dehorning or other routine procedures.

Making Medicine

That's how what is now the medicine coumarin (Warfarin) was discovered, and today, taken in careful doses, it's a life-saving one. Just don't feed moldy hay to your cows!

Lucky You!

Luck Has Nothing to Do with It

"Boy, you're good at finding four-leaf clovers!"

"Guess I must be extra lucky."

No, you're just good at recognizing patterns. Want to be extra lucky yourself? Start practicing!

Not Like the Others

That's what you're looking for when you hunt four-leaf clovers—a shape that's different than the others. At first, you'll have to consciously examine each clover to check. As a kid, I often laid on my belly to get a good view.

Get the Knack with Practice

After you find your first few four-leafers, that pattern will be imprinted in your brain, and you can simply scan rather than look at every clover.

Amaze Your Friends!

The more often you look for four-leaf clovers, the faster your pattern-recognizing brain will get the pattern down pat. Then you too can seem to be extra lucky, when you "just so happen" to look down and find a four-leaf clover, just like that!

Pattern Possibility

Each clover leaf has a lighter-colored V across it. When you're looking at a typical group of three leaves, those Vs form a triangular shape. In a clover with four leaves, they make a rectangle.

Seeing What We Don't See

I never noticed that triangle/rectangle consciously—or even the V on a clover leaf, for that matter—until someone pointed it out. But maybe my brain did. Give yours a try, and see how lucky you are!

Oriole nectar feeder

Let's Go Shopping...Again!

This time we're buying summer-blooming bulbs from catalogs or online, to plant now. The two big ones: lilies and gladiolus. (Lots of others, too, so enjoy your shopping!)

Any Spot Is a Good Spot

Lilies are gorgeous, anywhere you plant them. Splurge on a few fat bulbs, or a dozen, and plant them in pots or in your garden.

Start a Trend!

Glads are nowhere near as popular as they were back in the '50s and '60s. Time to bring them back! Glads have come a long way since the tall, stiff soldiers.

In with the New

New species and hybrids of glads are coming on the scene—shorter, arching, or half-height. Don't turn the catalog page at that word "glads"; these are easy and beautiful.

Embracing the Old

The old-fashioned (there's that word again!) tall, single-stemmed, stiffly upright glads are still worth finding a spot for. Those saturated colors and ruffly blossoms are fantastic—and hummingbirds agree.

So Much Beauty for So Little Money!

Gladiolus bulbs (they're technically corms) are sold in multiples, and they cost less than daffs or tulips—as little as $5.99 a dozen at big discount stores. Or you can shop specialty catalogs, where stupendous new varieties go for as much as $1 a bulb.

The Hardest Part?

Choosing your favorite color, of course! Glads come in every shade of the rainbow except true blue. You can even find green-flowered varieties!

Plant a Fountain

Graceful glads? The big ones? You bet! Just plant 3 or 5 corms, all one color, in the same hole. The outer ones will lean outward like a fountain; others will stand up straight.

Wow, Fireworks!

Or go for broke, and plant 12 gladiolus corms in one hole! Overall effect: An eye-popping splash of color if you use rich reds or purples, a romantic fountain with pastels.

Sore
Thumb

Softened

Stiff as a Soldier, or Softened?

Always plant glads—even the newer short varieties—in groups for a more natural effect. Tall glads stand out like a sore thumb if you dot them around, one here, one there. A spray of multiple bulbs is much softer—even if they're fire-engine red.

Ready for a Crowd

If you're refilling your hummingbird or oriole feeder frequently—once a day or more—save time by mixing up a
batch of sugar syrup: 1 part sugar to 1 part water. Store it
in your fridge, and at refill time, dilute it as needed.

Home Depot

Birds are adept at finding their own nest materials, but
some things are in scant supply, especially fibers for weav-
ing and lining nests, and fluff and feathers for softening
them.

Both females + male orioles
collect fibers to weave the nest.
Note how she loops the string
for easier carrying.

Best Customers

Drape 6–10" lengths of white cotton string over bushes or
on the lawn, and watch how fast it disappears! Do watch,
because you'll want to see the orioles that come to take it,
and it'll warm your heart to know robins have worked
your handout into their home.

Those Squirrels We Love...

Their antics aren't nearly as heartwarming in late spring,
when they raid birds' nests to eat eggs and nestlings.

Eggs & Meat

Jays and grackles share the same taste for eggs and nestlings, so they're raiding nests now, too. Not nice, in our view; perfectly natural behavior, to them.

Dropping Breakfast

Parent birds do their best to drive off nest raiders, often causing them to drop an egg or nestling that you may later find. Sadly, it's usually too late to rescue.

Radishes for Butterflies

Quick to grow, yummy to eat, and always some left-overs that go to flower about now. Let your blooming radishes stay: They're hugely popular with butterflies, and the green seedpods are spicy in salads.

Lettuce for Goldfinches

I don't mind at all when my lettuce bolts as the weather warms—it's a magnet for goldfinches. They'll alight on the stalks to pick off every fluffy seed.

Song Before Leaving

You've likely hosted white-throated sparrows all winter, and now it's time for them to go. When you hear their quavering *"Old Sam Peabiddy"* songs, get ready to say goodbye—those males are ready to start family life, far to the north.

Backwards Calendar

It's a lot easier to keep track of when birds arrive than it is to remember when they've left. Jot down the feeder guests on a calendar, so you notice right away when juncos or winter sparrows have departed.

Head Start

Tiger swallowtail butterflies are one of the best decorations of the late spring garden! These first swallowtails hatch from chrysalises that overwintered, and now they'll get started on laying eggs for two or three more broods to last the summer.

Tiger Swallowtail

GOODBYE TO SPRING

All of our resident birds are now at home with us, raising families. Migrants have gone on their way, and are doing the same in their homelands.

The garden is in full bloom, a pleasure to stroll every day. The vegetable garden is growing great guns, and we're enjoying the fruits (veggies!) of our labors. The sun is getting stronger, and summer is coming on.

What a wonderful spring it's been! We've watched it from the very first signs to full growth and bloom.

Sure hope you've enjoyed it as much as we have. And now it's time to just soak it all in, and think about how far we've come. See you in summer!